ROCK THIS TOWN!

DEDICATION

To Jules

AUTHOR'S NOTE

The events described in this book are based on my personal experience and are drawn from my memory, my collection of photos and press clippings, and from stories told to me. As Jules' wife, this is my life as I remember it. The passage of time has a tendency to distort memory. To ensure accuracy, I called on many people who provided invaluable assistance. They are listed in the acknowledgments at the end of the book. Many terrific people passed through our company, but I have chosen to introduce those people who have remained a part of our lives.

©2018 Fran Belkin www.franprojects.com

ISBN: 978-1-7326933-0-2

Book Design by Christopher Hixson
Typeset primarily in Museo family, designed by Jos Buivenga
Manufactured in the United States of America by Worzalla

34567890

ROCK THIS TOWN!

Backstage in Cleveland:
Stories you never heard & swag you never saw

Fran Belkin

with CHRISTOPHER HIXSON

Foreword by BARRY GABEL

FRANPROJECTS

Concert promoter Jules Belkin backstage with shock-rock group Twisted Sister, Richfield Coliseum, January 28, 1986 ©Anastasia Pantsios

Rock and roll fans know all about what was happening on the concert stage.

What was going on backstage was an entirely different story.

"Twisted Sister was waiting in the stairwell for their encore, and I overheard one of the guys say to lead singer Dee Snyder, 'I don't know how much longer I can do this.' Dee grinned and replied, 'But listen to all that money out there.' *Tom Einhouse, former Belkin runner*

Lynyrd Skynyrd on stage at the first World Series of Rock, Cleveland Municipal Stadium, June 23, 1974 ©Janet Macoska

They told me I was going to have to work for a living
But all I want to do is ride.
I don't care where we're going from here. Honey, you decide.
— Jackson Browne, The Road & Sky

Foreword

Everyone remembers their first concert. Think about it.

Here in Cleveland, the mere mention of The World Series of Rock is etched in the minds of anyone who attended. Bruce at the Allen Theatre... Michael Stanley at Blossom... whoever, wherever. *You remember it, right?* The energy, the overwhelming excitement of the crowd, the anticipation of the band taking the stage and the hit song you still sing. When you hear that song on the radio you're instantly transported back to that concert, to that time like none other you have ever experienced except for the birth of your kids or the joint you didn't inhale.

This book is a love letter to the people who purchased a ticket, who worked the shows, who got the band from one town to the next, who have their own memories etched in their souls. But mostly this is a love letter that Fran wanted to share with the world about her incredible life with Jules.

"They told me I was going to have to work for a living"...and interestingly, my "work" turned out to be the memory-making business. Yes, I've sold a few concert tickets and sponsorships along the way to stay in the game, but truth be told, I too am a prisoner of rock and roll!

Jules and Mike Belkin were rock and roll trailblazers in every sense of the word. They worked incredibly hard, risking their financial lives at every turn with no North Star to guide them. The duo collected friends from around the world and across the street—from every walk of life. They provided careers for countless people behind the scenes, as well as nurtured the careers of some of the most influential artists that shaped the entertainment industry and live music landscape.

If you live and breathe music like I do, you're about to be transported back to that magical time with every turn of the page. As it's been said, every picture tells a story.

Barry Gabel

Belkin Productions
Present
FRANK ZAP
& THE MOTHE
OF INVENTI

SPECIAL GUEST: Robin Tr

SUN. DEC. 1
Public H

TICKET
$550 ADV. $650

TICKETS ON SALE NOW
PUBLIC HALL BOX OFFICE
ALL CLEVELAND TUX SHOPS, WARD'S FOLLY

Recalling days when rock rolled, Mickey Berkowitz and Fran Belkin wear be-glittered T-shirts with messages.

The white platform shoes may have gone out of style, but rock and roll t-shirts never will. Fran poses with Mickey Berkowitz of Ward's Folly clothing store, an early ticketing location for Belkin shows. Cleveland Plain Dealer, September 9, 1973. A 1974 poster for Frank Zappa's show at Cleveland Public Hall.

Introduction

My husband Jules and his brother Mike started Belkin Productions in 1966. It began as a lark—booking and promoting the occasional concert in Cleveland—but it grew quickly and by the early '70s was their full-time enterprise. Thanks to great timing, good luck and the birth of rock music, Belkin Productions and Cleveland became a powerhouse in the national music scene for the next 35 years. Our lives changed forever, throwing us into a world of high intensity and adrenaline, riding the tidal wave of the music and concerts, mingling with musicians on their way up and lucky to shake their hands once they were famous. It was always exciting, and our lives had a vigor and energy that astonished us.

In 2001 SFX Entertainment began buying top-tier local promotion companies, consolidating them into one huge national entity which would eventually become Live Nation. The name Belkin Productions, once prominent on every regional concert ad, ticket and poster, vanished.

My collection of t-shirts chronicling the golden days of Cleveland rock and roll wound up in boxes in the attic, until one day I realized those shirts illustrated the incredible journey of our family business. They are the 'spine' of the story I wanted to share with our grandchildren, who were all under seven when the company was sold.

Band t-shirts have always been a big part of rock and roll. A shirt broadcast to the world that you were there and saw the show live. The shirts were, and are, status symbols that have become timeless memorabilia. Shirts showcase custom artwork, tour dates and cities, opening the door for strangers to become friends. "How many shows did *you* see?" "Which cities?" "How about that version of XXX they played?" "Can't wait for the next tour!"

Selling t-shirts, sweatshirts and caps is big business. Merchandise is sold at every show, by the box and sometimes by the truckload, to fans lined up to take home a talisman of the experience.

But in the early days of rock and roll, there were other t-shirts being made that never got into the hands of the fans.

These were t-shirts that were custom-made for a specific concert, in small quantities, and hand-presented to the bands and their crew by the promoter. Why, you might ask. To engender loyalty in a fiercely competitive, cut-throat business and to thank them for multiple dates, a small token of appreciation for the chance to reap a box office bonanza.

As Belkin Productions started booking multiple dates on bands' tours, we would design shirts for the band and crew as gifts—better known as 'swag'. The bigger the band, the bigger the tour, the better the swag. When the crew arrived early in the morning to load in the show, aside from "Where's the coffee?" they'd ask our promoter rep, "Where's the Belkin swag?" or "Is our swag gonna be as cool as when I was here with the Stones?"

Jules personally selected the swag. Then the graphic artist gave us a fun and unique design. We weren't looking to design shirts like the band's in-your-face merchandise, we were about being subtle and high concept. No piece of swag went out the door without the Belkin Productions logo. To the bands, it was swag, but to us, it reinforced our presence as one of the premier promoters in the country.

One question we're still asked time and again: "Did you become friends with any of the rock stars?" The truth is that we worked *for* the stars, just like their managers, agents and touring staff. Those were our friends, with whom we had something in common. Our goal, and theirs, was to produce the best concert every single night, and we did.

These T-shirts and stories take you on a tour of my life, the unique relationships and amazing personalities that shaped Belkin Productions, the concert industry and my fortunate and remarkable journey with my husband Jules, an exceptional man in all ways.

And, most importantly, this is the story I want to tell.

Fran Belkin, Cleveland 2018

'This is the story I want to tell.'

The author backstage at a
1977 World Series of Rock concert,
Cleveland, Ohio

Baseball jersey-style t-shirt, 1972

So, how do we book a concert?

With one question, the Belkin brothers went from selling menswear to securing their place center stage in the musical *and* cultural revolution.

Jules, with brother Mike on stage at Cleveland Public Hall, May 14, 1969 Photo: Cleveland Plain Dealer

It was a great first question from Mike and Jules Belkin when the duo first dipped their toes into concert promotion in 1965. But let's not get ahead of a story that actually begins in 1931.

Classical and jazz were the popular music of the day, and *Brother Can You Spare A Dime?* was the number one song in a country mired in the Great Depression. On the brighter side, RCA released the first commercially-issued 33 1/3 rpm record. And Jules debuted hot on its heels. By the time brother Mike arrived in 1935, Fred Astaire's recording of *Cheek to Cheek* was sitting atop the popular charts. Still, another fifteen years would pass before the term "Rock and Roll" was coined by Alan Freed, and the Moondog Coronation Ball in Cleveland went down in history as the first rock concert.

Jules graduated from University of Michigan in January 1953, and came back to Cleveland to work in his dad's men's clothing store at West 25th and Clark. At that time, every able-bodied man had to serve in the armed forces for two years. He enlisted in June of 1954, was sent first to Fort Knox, KY for Basic Training and then the south side of Chicago working in the Medical Corps administrative office of the 5th Army. In his spare time (and to make a few bucks) he bartended at the Officer's Club and enjoyed it so much, he also took a job in a local bar. His talent for mixing drinks surfaced at this time, as did his talent for drinking them.

Jules came back to Cleveland in 1956 and again worked for his father, Sam, while attending law school at night. Two years later, Sam had a heart attack. He survived, but started to work less. Jules dropped out of law school to help.

Mike graduated, got married and joined the business, too. This made expansion possible. Jules took over major responsibility for Belkin's Mens Shop while Mike became involved in discount stores in Painesville and Ashtabula.

In April 1962, Jules was set up with a girl from LA who was visiting relatives in Cleveland. They went on two dates, but she had to return to finish classes at UCLA. A month later he cashed in his meager savings, flew to LA and proposed. She said yes, and by July that same year, Jules and Fran were married.

The owner of the Ashtabula store was booking big band orchestras to play on the weekend and offering half price tickets as a way to drive traffic to his store. The concerts were quite successful, but he got tired of the booking, and in 1965 asked Mike to take it over.

Mike started talking to agents in New York and when they found out he was from Cleveland, they asked why he wasn't booking music in Cleveland instead of Ashtabula. The brothers decided to test the concert waters and booked The New Christy Minstrels and the Four Freshmen for Cleveland Music Hall in February 1966.

Sam with Jules on his wedding day, 1962

Pola, Jules and Steve at the West 25th Street office, 1969

Proud parents

Sam wasn't too enthusiastic about this new business, and he never got the chance to see how successful his sons would become. Sam passed away in 1966. Their mother, Pola, loved picking up the paper and seeing "Belkin Productions Presents" in the ads. While most of the shows didn't appeal to her, she didn't miss the sold-out Frank Sinatra concert at Public Hall in 1969, beaming with pride at the accomplishments of her boys. She passed away later that year.

AMUSEMENTS
AMUSEMENTS
BELKIN & ANDERSON
PRESENT
THE NEW CHRISTY MINSTRELS
WITH THE FOUR FRESHMEN
FIRST CLEVELAND SHOWING
Never before on the same stage
MUSIC HALL
2 great shows Saturday, February 5 7:30 and 10 P.M.
TICKETS $3, $4, $5
Advance sale at Burrows, 419 Euclid and all branches. Mail Orders Accepted. Enclose stamped, self-addressed envelope. Please specify performance.

"We'd have to sell a lot of socks to make $59, so it looked pretty good to us."

—Jules and Mike on the meager profits from the first show, February 5, 1966

Then they had to ask the questions: *Where do you sell tickets? How do you make up an ad for the newspaper? What kind of insurance do you need? How to deal with the Stagehands union? Security guards?* They had so much confidence in the lineup they booked two shows on the same night. The shows didn't do well, and they lost over $400, but they were loathe to admit it. Instead, publicly they said they made $59.

The next show Mike booked was The Mamas & the Papas, the new hot group. The band canceled twice, citing illness, and the show never happened. The brothers said,

"That's it. We are done with the music business!"

Shortly after that, they got a call from radio station WJW saying jazz impresario George Wein was looking to do a festival in Cleveland and wanted to know who the local promoter was. The brothers recognized the name and knew this guy was the real deal. They decided to work with George.

George liked the old Cleveland Arena at 36th and Euclid as a venue for the Jazz Festival. In the meantime, riots erupted in the Hough area of Cleveland, resulting in a divided community. There were concerns prior to the concert because the audience for jazz was both black and white.

The day before the Jazz Fest sales were looking pretty bleak. Jules went to Richman Brothers at Severance Mall, where his tickets were being sold and saw a line to get into the store. He thought, "They must be having a big sale." When he walked inside, he realized all those people in line were jazz fans buying tickets on the payday closest to the show.

What a night in Cleveland for the Jazz Festival! Sarah Vaughn, Horace Silver, Miles Davis and others, an all star lineup, with the audience enjoying the music....the brothers finally made a profit and they were back in business.

The next show (November 1966) was Andy Warhol and the Velvet Underground at Music Hall, and what an audience they brought! Kids coming to that show were wearing bell bottom pants and had long hair. It was the first time Jules and Mike had seen 'hippies' in person. The *Summer of Love* was still a year away, but the counter culture was rising.

As the mother of a friend remarked,"We sent him to college with a crew cut and khakis, and he came home with long hair and bell bottoms!"

The country was in the midst of a culture shift... opposition to the Vietnam war, the Civil Rights movement, and the Beatles. Long hair, free music and free love, that was what everyone wanted. Marching against the war, marching for civil rights and attending huge rock concerts quickly became the focus of a generation.

It was surreal; in 1967 the brothers booked 13 shows, and in 1968 they booked 43. Rock and roll was taking off, and they were in the middle of the vortex.

"Things were looking scary."

—Jules recalling ticket sales for the jazz festival just weeks following the riots

It was a steamy night in the old Arena. You could feel the love of the audience as Miles Davis performed, sweating in the heat, pouring his heart into the music. He was one of my favorites, so it was quite thrilling to be standing in the wings of the stage watching him play. As he came off the stage, he walked toward me, smiling. I couldn't believe it, would he actually talk to me? I was beaming as he came up to me and said softly, "Hey babe, you wanna fuck?" I was so shocked I couldn't answer, my red face said it all. He chuckled and walked away.
Fran Belkin

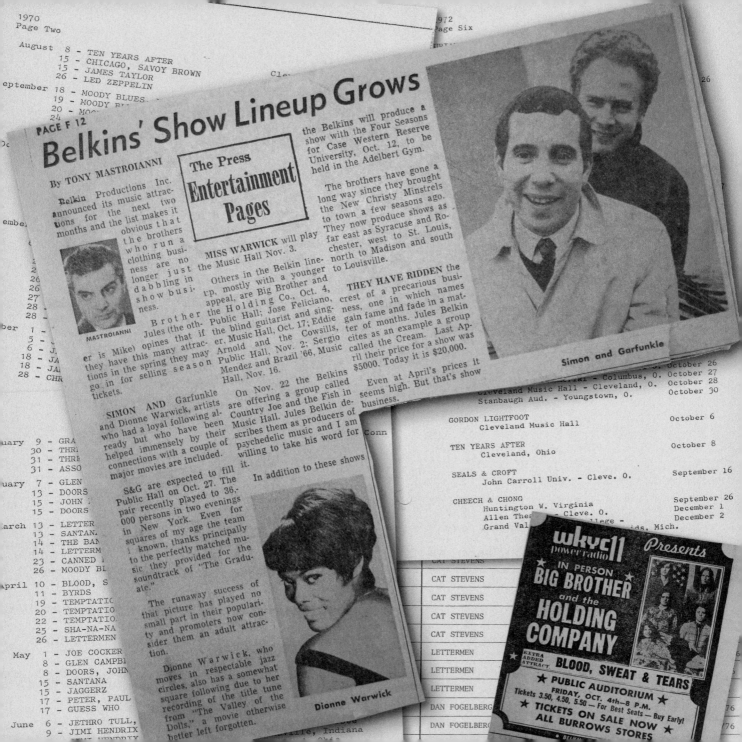

Agents kept calling and asking, *"What about this city? Detroit? Cincinnati? Louisville? Syracuse? Rochester? St. Louis?"*

It was a thrilling time and a scary time as they learned everything by trial and error. They were vilified in the underground newspaper because they were charging for tickets: the music belonged to the people and they should get it for free. But Mike and Jules were more concerned with how to manage so many concerts as they expanded into more cities. They were also working with lots of new bands: Jimi Hendrix, the Doors, the Four Seasons, Simon and Garfunkel, and Cream.

In 1969, they promoted 86 shows in 26 cities. Now there were shows from Michigan to North Carolina, New York to Minnesota. They premiered Led Zeppelin, as well as Blood, Sweat and Tears, Sly and the Family Stone, Jefferson Airplane. Mike, who was no longer involved with the stores in Painesville and Ashtabula, was booking rock, folk, jazz, blues, acts as diverse as Sonny & Cher, Johnny Mathis, Johnny Carson, the Lettermen, the Temptations, Crosby, Stills and Nash, and

"Nobody but Jimi burns a house down."

—Jimi, in response to the bomb scare during his March 26, 1968 concert at Cleveland Public Hall

Jules (left) escorts Jimi Hendrix past excited fans in downtown Cleveland, March 1968

★ Belkin Productio
Presents A . . .
CONCERT THA
WILL TAKE YO
ON A MOST
EXCITING TRIP
WITH

JIMI HENDRIX

PUBLIC HALL
SAT., SEPT. 6, 8 P.M
ALL SEATS RESERVED
$4 • $5 • $6
TICKETS ON SALE TOMORROW
At All Burrows Stores
AND
Cleveland Convention Center
Box Office

...VE with JIMI

"And suddenly there is Janis exploding in "Piece of My Heart"...her gutsy, bluesy voice coming across like a tornado in a hurricane."

—Jane Scott, Plain Dealer music critic, October 5, 1968

Janis Joplin (solo, she had left Big Brother and the Holding Company). Jules was doing the advertising, ticket sales and production and traveling to many of the out-of-town shows—and running the clothing store.

By this time, Jules and Mike had started putting together partnerships with local guys in the different cities they worked. Mike would book the show and the hall, then Jules would work with the local person to place advertising, sell tickets and do the production. For example, in Madison, Wisconsin, Jules partnered with Herb Frank, who ran the ticketing agency for the arena there. Herb knew how to sell the tickets, place the advertising and perform basic production duties. Usually Jules would go for night of show, but sometimes there were multiple shows in one night, so he looked to people like Herb Frank to do the settlement and pay the band.

Another important partnership was developing. Clair Brothers Sound had a beginning similar to the Belkin brothers. In 1966, the Four Seasons had played a gig in Miami, opening for Herb Alpert and the Tijuana Brass. The Brass had their own sound system and wouldn't let anyone use it. The Four Seasons had to use a funky house system and decided they needed their own sound too. Their next stop was a university gig in Lancaster, PA, where Roy and Gene Clair were the house sound company. They were two guys from Lititz, PA, just out of high school, who were developing sound systems. Frankie Valli liked their system so much, he hired them on the spot and asked them to come to Cleveland for his next gig.

In Cleveland, the Clair brothers met the Belkin brothers, and they immediately recognized their shared interests. The Belkins asked them to provide the sound at Cleveland Public Hall and Music Hall. Mike also hired Clair Brothers to do the sound for the James Gang. Mike and Jules would recommend the Clairs to bands when they played Cleveland. When YES played Public Hall, they hired Roy to go on tour with them, followed by the Moody Blues. The major bands started using Clair Bros. sound, which meant the supporting acts had to use them too—introducing them to up and coming bands, who in turn would use Clair when they became the headliners.

While audiences grooved to their favorite bands, the two sets of brothers worked backstage, still in amazement at the size, scope and potential of the concert business.

By 1970, the Clairs had designed and built the first stage monitor, and in 1972 they installed the first hanging sound system for an indoor arena—

Above: Mike and Jules at the family store, c. 1972
Jules at the first office of Belkin Productions, c. 1972
Bottom: Roy Clair of Clair Brothers sound, c. 1977

In the early '70s, Jules was covering Sonny & Cher shows throughout the Midwest. After the Cleveland concert, the tour manager offered Jules and Fran seats on their private jet to Indianapolis for the next night's show. They happily accepted.

The next day, the tour manager asked if they wanted to come to a movie with the band and crew. The theater was empty... they had bought all the seats so Sonny and Cher could watch the film undisturbed!

Fran says "I got you, Babe."

❝ Cher was wearing this super cool studded denim jacket and pants outfit—custom made, for sure. Joking, I asked her if I could have it when she was done with it. She replied, 'Ha, in your dreams! But if you really want it, you can get it yourself at Fred Segal in LA". The following month we were in Los Angeles, and I made a bee line to Fred Segal's store and sure enough, they had the exact same outfit. I still wear the jacket (pants, no). **❞** *Fran Belkin*

no more stacks of speakers filling the stage and blocking concert-goers sight-lines. Clair Companies is now one of the largest sound companies in the world; it designs and installs permanent sound systems worldwide while still touring with major acts around the world. Clair Brothers and Belkin Productions were always intertwined both professionally and personally. Today, Roy Clair and Jules remain great friends.

But there was another VERY important partnership. Cleveland was ahead of the curve in the music revolution. And why was that? RADIO! Innovative disc jockeys and program directors, and the eventual advent of FM radio. In the '60s it was WIXY, with jocks like Billy Bass, who sought out and played new bands. When FM took over, WMMS was playing albums, introducing new music to their listeners and creating demand for the live concerts Belkin was booking. WMMS and Belkin would co-promote a concert, and their jocks would go onstage in front of thousands of screaming fans to introduce the band, turning them into local celebrities, too. The jocks worked hard to stay in front of the trends and be the first in the country to play the next big hit. Visiting bands always wanted to go on 'MMS and do interviews to promote their shows, and the station was only too happy to have world-famous musicians cross their threshold. WMMS had become one of the most important and imitated stations in the country.

After 500 concerts, it was time to choose: Fill stadiums or sell suits?

Around this time, the brothers moved their office from the rental tuxedo storage room at the back of the store. In their new office at 30th and Euclid, Mike now had room for his two rapidly growing companies, Sweet City Records and Belkin Personal Management, which he had started with Carl Maduri. In addition to handling advertising *and* production, Jules began to take over the concert booking. It was a juggling act, and it was time to choose....

Jules realized he couldn't continue to grow the concert business while also running the store. So in 1972, they sold the store and were full time in the music business.

Another juggling act was being played out at Playhouse Square in downtown Cleveland. By the early 1970s, the theaters in Playhouse Square were slated for demolition, because the owners felt it would be more profitable to have the land for parking lots. In 1972, Belkin Productions started booking rock concerts in the Allen Theatre. Only rock music could draw audiences into that old dilapidated theater. The kids loved going there because they didn't have to behave like they did at the fancier Music Hall. It was small and intimate and had great sound. They could stand on the seats,

Bowie's U.S. debut at the 3,000-seat Cleveland Music Hall quickly sold out, but the rest of his first tour wasn't as successful (in San Francisco, only a few hundred people showed up). Bowie came back to Cleveland six weeks later and sold out the 10,000-seat Public Hall for two nights. The constant airplay on WMMS helped launch his career in the U.S., and Cleveland became one of his favorite tour stops.

David Bowie, Cleveland Public Hall, June 18, 1974 ©Janet Macoska

"I was program director at WMMS and we'd just gone through the Woodstock and Altamont era. To keep our underdog, alternative status and separate us from the Southern Rock sound, I needed something new and alternative to play. I listened to Bowie's *Hunky Dory* album, and I said, 'This is it!' I put it into heavy rotation." *Billy Bass*

Jules, the Divine Miss M, and the publicity stunt that packed the house.

Jules wasn't familiar with Bette Midler or her act, but on the advice of her agent (and my friend Judie in LA) he took a chance and booked her for a winter '73 show at Music Hall. He knew the show would need good press coverage to sell well, so he devised a publicity stunt.

Jules hired a bikini model, rented a fake palm tree, and had a few signs made. Then, he borrowed my convertible, put the top down, and drove back and forth on snow-dusted Euclid Avenue with the shivering girl posing and waving at the passersby—and the reporters he'd called. The stunt did the trick and a photo made the front page of the next day's Cleveland Press. The show quickly sold out.

On the day of the show, Jules met Bette for the first time when he accompanied her to a radio interview. After she was out of ear shot in the sound booth, Jules called me.

"Fran, I hope I didn't make a mistake," he said. "She's this shy little homely thing with her hat pulled down tight over her head..."

That night, Bette walked on stage and Jules' jaw dropped. The ugly duckling had transformed into a swan, her smile lighting up the theater. She sang, she danced, she told jokes and she vamped all over the stage until we were doubled over with laughter.

And she had a terrific music director named Barry Manilow.*

Once wasn't enough, and fortunately Jules had booked her a few nights later in Columbus. So a group of us rented a van and drove down to see the show again. I regret we didn't make her a shirt, because once she became popular she started performing at Blossom Music Center, where we didn't book the shows.

*Manilow later enjoyed solo success, and his rider came with an unusual request: "No one looks at Barry when he leaves his dressing room. Everyone is to face the wall until he is on stage."

Barry Manilow & Bette Midler at Swingo's, January 20, 1973
©George Shuba

BELKIN PRODUCTIONS & WMMS PRESENTS
The Devine Miss M, Bette Midler, Is This Year's Musical Superstar. Sold Out Concert Engagements Throughout The Country. She's an "entertainer" with an "act" but what an act! Her singing — try Streisand, Garland, Piaf, Andrews Sisters ... incredible! Her live show can't be fully described, let alone captured on record!

YOU'VE SEEN HER ON THE JOHNNY CARSON SHOW!

Bette Midler

MUSIC HALL • JAN. 20th • 7:30 P.M.
ALL SEATS RESERVED $4.50 ADVANCE — $5.50 DAY OF SHOW
TICKETS ON SALE NOW! PUBLIC HALL BOX OFFICE
ALL CLEVE. TUX SHOPS, WARD'S FOLLY & SARTORIUM

dance in the aisles and spill beer on the floor. It was the perfect rock and roll theater.

Belkin Productions continued to book shows and pay rent, which made the owners realize the theaters still had value. Pollstar (the trade publication for the concert industry) named the Allen as one of the best rock venues in the nation. The Allen Theatre premiered many of rock's biggest names on their way up, including Roxy Music, ZZ Top, Genesis, and Kiss. Bruce Springsteen opened for Wishbone Ash and then came back the next year as the headliner. Eventually Belkin expanded the bookings to include the Palace Theatre. This was one of the catalysts which kept the pulse beating and helped drive Playhouse Square's eventual renaissance.

By the early '70s, the demand for the music was so great, there weren't large enough indoor venues. It was time to rock the stadiums...

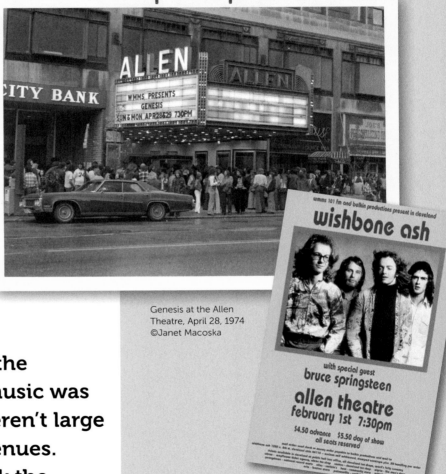

Genesis at the Allen Theatre, April 28, 1974
©Janet Macoska

BELKIN PRODUCTIONS

AKRON RUBBER BOWL

"The fourth concert of the season was the Rolling Stones, with Stevie Wonder opening. Early in the show, the cops came down the aisle toward the stage en masse in a show of force. Fortunately, Stevie couldn't see them and he just kept on playing without missing a note!" *Jules Belkin*

In the summer of '72, all hell broke loose ...and we had the time of our lives!

Belkin Productions started producing outdoor concerts at the Akron Rubber Bowl, which held 32,000 people. Jules and the staff had to learn hands-on, and quickly, the logistics of securing large venues, the impact of weather, and all the unexpected problems associated with shows of this magnitude.

One of the first shows, Chicago, wasn't selling well. Just before show time, the sky opened up and the rain poured. And poured. The simple canvas tarp roof over the stage sagged from the weight of the water and the entire roof collapsed just before the show started! Jules had to cancel the show, and concertgoers were told to save their tickets for a rescheduled date.

By the time the new date arrived, Chicago had released a hugely popular album and the show sold out immediately. People showed up with their tickets from the first show that had been soaked at the time and it was almost impossible to read them. We'll never know how many people gained entry with an old piece of warped card stock.

The Akron cops hated rock and roll, and at the slightest provocation would throw tear gas at the kids. They made it so unpleasant, the Belkins stayed only one summer.

Akron Rockfest Clash Deflate

Akron Police Capt. John Stroh disclaimed yesterday any talk of a riot at the Rolling Stones Concert. The momentary violence at the beginning of the concert at the Rubber Bowl resulted in only two arrests, he said.

Although nearly 30 persons were arrested on a number of minor charges during the several hours before and during the concert, the fracas that brought police into the stadium in force was quickly subdued and did not result in large scale arrests, Stroh said.

STROH WAS in charge of the police force at the concert Tuesday.

The incident started over

an attempted drug arrest. The police were ignoring the use of marijuana, which was widespread. But Lt. John Lower said he saw a young man apparently selling a "white powdery substance."

Lower tried to collar the man. The man struck at Lower and ran down the stadium stairs into the grass.

AS LOWER chased the suspect, another man hit Lower and he fell, dragging the suspect to the ground. At the same time, other police and members of the audience became involved in the altercation.

The police used billy

clubs and a chemical spra The others used feet, roc and beer cans. The ruck brought about 50 police or the grounds, who rushed t crowd and then retreated.

After that violence th rest of the evening passe without incident, except fo a normal number of ove doses and individual obstr perousness.

"That was no riot," Str said. "We had a little tro ble earlier in the day wh the kids stormed the co don. We decided to let the in, and they didn't cause trouble. For the most pa they were pretty well haved."

Plain Dealer,
July 13, 1972

> Doing concerts at the Rubber Bowl was really fun and exciting. We hadn't done big shows like this before. It was a huge undertaking, and we were learning as we went along. *Jules Belkin*

1972 RUBBER BOWL CONCERT SERIES

June 16	Three Dog Night • James Gang	**August 5**	Alice Cooper • Dr. John • J. Geils Band
June 24	Black Sabbath • Humble Pie • Ramatam • Edgar Winter	**August 11**	Yes • Mahavishnu Orchestra • Eagles
July 3	Faces with Rod Stewart • Badfinger	**August 18**	Allman Bros Band (Cancelled)
July 11	The Rolling Stones • Stevie Wonder	**August 20**	Chicago (originally scheduled for July 9th)
July 21	Osmond Brothers • The Heywoods • Jan Baker	**August 21**	Jefferson Airplane • Commander Cody • Hot Tuna

'It was one big tear gas scene!'

Jules Belkin

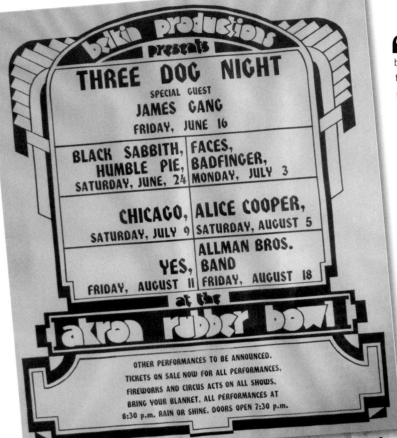

belkin productions presents

THREE DOG NIGHT
SPECIAL GUEST
JAMES GANG
FRIDAY, JUNE 16

BLACK SABBITH, HUMBLE PIE,
SATURDAY, JUNE, 24

FACES, BADFINGER,
MONDAY, JULY 3

CHICAGO,
SATURDAY, JULY 9

ALICE COOPER,
SATURDAY, AUGUST 5

YES,
FRIDAY, AUGUST 11

ALLMAN BROS. BAND
FRIDAY, AUGUST 18

at the

akron rubber bowl

OTHER PERFORMANCES TO BE ANNOUNCED.
TICKETS ON SALE NOW FOR ALL PERFORMANCES,
FIREWORKS AND CIRCUS ACTS ON ALL SHOWS,
BRING YOUR BLANKET, ALL PERFORMANCES AT
8:30 p.m. RAIN OR SHINE, DOORS OPEN 7:30 p.m.

"Jefferson Airplane hit the stage and all hell broke loose. Halfway into their set, I suddenly felt like someone was choking me and gouging my eyes out at the same time. The police had teargassed some kids at the top of the bowl, and the gas settled on the field below where a few thousand of us were blissfully unaware of the small riot going on nearby. Next thing I knew, someone on stage was urging us to "attack the pigs," and then the show was over.

The Akron Beacon Journal broke the details to our parents the next day: 27 had been arrested, including singer Grace Slick for assaulting an officer. Fellow Airplane member Paul Kantner (the article called him "her old man") was also arrested."
Tim Quine, Rubber City Review

"They played the greatest rock 'n' roll music all night, and now they're telling the kids that there's more to life than music. The Stones are telling the kids to go out and make this a better world to live in." *Billy Bass*

Cleveland Press,
July 12, 1972

Magnificent Mick wows Stones fans

By BRUNO BORNINO

The Rolling Stones' concert in the Akron Rubber Bowl last night was supposed to be THE rock 'n' roll show for the summer of '72. And it was.

In fact, it probably was the best rock show since the Beatles performed in the Stadium in 1966.

Magnificent Mick Jagger — the legendary leader of the Stones — was every-

ly-lighted stage. He was the purple people pleaser.

One young girl near the front of the stage jumped up with a big sign that read ORGASM.

Jagger, who couldn't miss seeing the sign, showed a toothy grin and continued with his constant-motion performance. He thoroughly enjoys being rock music's main sex symbol.

Girls idolize him, so guys envy him. He's No. 1 in the

girls near the edge of the stage.

Jagger also plays harmonica during this 10-minute rocker, and finally puts on one of his trademarks — a red, white and blue Uncle Sam top hat.

The crowd crushed forward and moved a wooden fence in front of the stage, but a menacing Jagger look and a gesture for them to

back off was immediately obeyed.

Jagger rewarded his huge following by going into a tune they were shouting for all night, "Jumping Jack Flash."

Greatest response came from another tune that was banned from the radio, "Street Fightin' Man."

Billy Bass, program director and general manager of radio station WMMS, said

"That makes it a perfect show."

Bass, one of Cleveland's top rock authorities, said, "They played the greatest rock 'n' roll music all night, and now they're telling the kids that there's more to life than music.

"The Stones are telling the kids to go out and do something to make this a better world to live in."

The brothers decided to try Cloverleaf Speedway by the Ohio & Erie Canal as an outdoor venue for the summer of '73. The track in bucolic Valley View, Ohio was usually home to stock car races, but the center field would make a fine concert venue. There wasn't much on-site parking, but there was a huge lot across the canal so they had a bridge constructed so people could walk over from the parking lot.

The traffic was so horrific on opening night that even the headliner Deep Purple couldn't get through to the Speedway and were over an hour late. Billy Preston opened the show and walked through the audience playing with his keyboard strapped around his neck to appease the impatient crowd. By the following day, the township was impatient too and pulled the permits for any future shows. After just one concert, the Cloverleaf concert "series" had ended.

> **"** I was the only one of my friends with a ticket, because I was the only one with a job. I came with two buddies and told them to wait outside the fence. After I got through the gate, I took off my shirt and rolled it up into a tight ball with the ticket inside and threw it back over the fence to my friend. He got through, and then he threw it over again for the other friend. I didn't know then that I'd one day marry the Belkins' daughter! **"** *Jerry Mizer*

A few months later, we made our first shirt for a specific band/show

THE HOME OF THE World Series of Rock

AEROS[MITH]
TODD RUN[DGREN]
LYNYRD S[KYNYRD]
EMERSO[N]
& [MORE]
TED N[UGENT]
PINK FLOYD
J. GEILS BAND
AND MORE!!

wmms 101 fm

IN CO-OPERATION WITH
BELKIN
PRODUCTIONS

the WORLD SERIES OF ROCK

CLEVELAND STADIUM

wmms 101 fm

Tokyo Shapiro

BELKIN PRODUCTIONS

❛ I'm a year out

BELKIN
PRODUCTIONS
presents
the WORLD OF SERIES ROCK
SUMMER of '74
CLEVELAND STADIUM

In '74, Jules and Mike took a shot at booking Cleveland Municipal Stadium, never dreaming they could eventually fill it with more than 80,000 screaming fans at multi-act, all day concerts that would wind up seared into the psyches of a generation of music fans. These shows were bigger than any ballgame, and the closest thing to hosting a World Series that Cleveland would get for decades.

But it was difficult to book the stadium. The Belkins had to work around the Cleveland Indians schedule *and* a band's touring schedule. They needed at least seven free days (four to five for set-up and a day after the show to tear down). An event this big needed a really great shirt and advertising concepts that would strike a chord with music fans. Jules liked the design of the recently introduced WMMS buzzard logo, so he called its young illustrator.

WMMS 101·FM

BELKIN PRODUCTIONS *presents*

Tokyo Shapiro

the WORLD OF SERIES ROCK
SUMMER of '74
CLEVELAND STADIUM

SUN. JUNE 23 2:00 P.M. DOORS OPEN at 12:30 P.M.

BEACH BOYS

JOE WALSH and BARNSTORM

SPECIAL GUESTS

LYNYRD SKYNYRD

REO SPEED WAGON

TICKETS: $7 ADVANCE $8 AT GATE
ENTRANCE AT GATE A & B

$ THOUSANDS $ of DOLLARS in AUDIO EQUIPMENT T-SHIRTS and RECORD ALBUMS to be given away FREE! During Concert!

★ SEATING ON FIELD OR IN STANDS! ★
★ PERFORMANCE GUARANTEED! — COME RAIN OR SHINE! ★

TICKETS ON SALE NOW AT THESE OUTLETS: PUBLIC HALL BOX OFFICE, ALL CLEVELAND TUX SHOPS, WARD'S FO'LY — Coventry — AKRON, Mayflower Ticket Agency, Akron Tux Shop • CANTON, Cleveland Tux Shop • ELYRIA • The Men's Shop • YOUNGSTOWN • NILES • National Record Mart • ERIE • Boston Store • KENT, Community Store • ASHTABULA, Schaffer & Sons. — IN COLUMBUS AT ALL CENTRAL TICKET OUTLETS AND IN TOLEDO AT THE SPORTS ARENA.

NO BOTTLES OR CANS ALLOWED IN STADIUM : INFO CALL (216) 696-1043

> **"** Jules contacted me through WMMS and asked if I would do some art. I was working at American Greetings, so I had to meet him after work. I'm a year out of art school and don't know shit, but I was able to come up with the idea and Jules liked it. The hand-drawn black and white art looked pretty crude and underground comix-like, but it worked. Jules was very patient with an inexperienced artist. **"** *David Helton*

# of art school and don't know shit. **"**
David Helton, illustrator

Backstage at the World Series of Rock

Building the stage and preparing the stadium for the show was the first priority. But what about backstage where the bands would be hanging out? When Jules realized there were no dressing rooms near the ramp to the stage, a plan had to be devised. What was there? Concrete floors and walls, damp, dark corridors, and old, ugly bathrooms.

Jules and Mike backstage

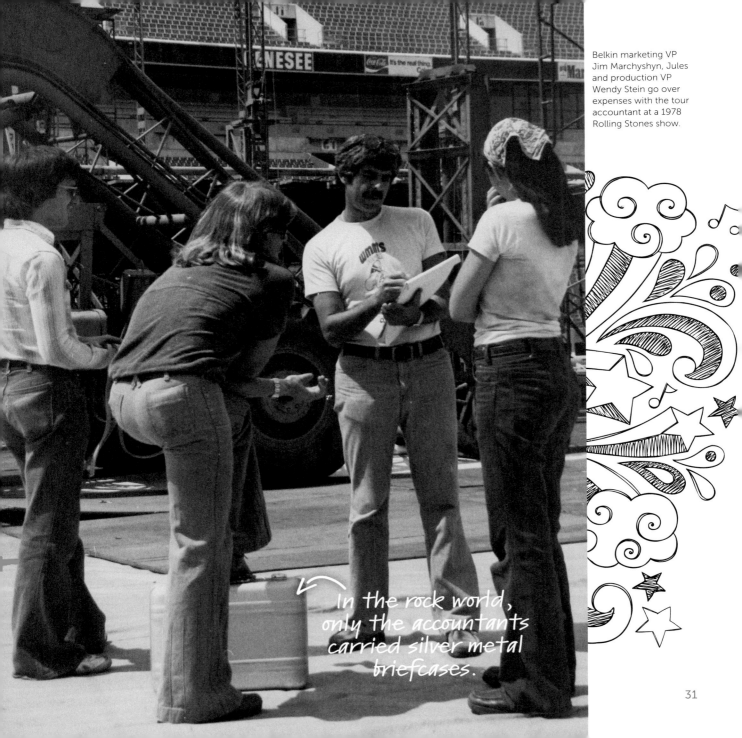

Belkin marketing VP Jim Marchyshyn, Jules and production VP Wendy Stein go over expenses with the tour accountant at a 1978 Rolling Stones show.

In the rock world, only the accountants carried silver metal briefcases.

Fran & niece Lisa Belkin
beautify the RVs

From concrete corridor to an alternative universe

Jules found a guy in Cuyahoga Falls who had a dealership full of recreational vehicles that he agreed to rent for dressing rooms. The RV's were driven into the concourse adjacent to the stage and arranged in a semi-circle for privacy. Wendy outlined the area with a truckload of rented plants, and gave the space a warm ambiance by installing carpeting, furniture, fountains and even decorative streetlights in the center of the temporary backstage village.

We stocked each RV with snacks, soft and hard drinks, towels and flowers. The personalized street sign out front let each band know which RV was theirs, so when they arrived they felt welcomed and respected. We created an unusual ambiance not normally seen backstage, instead of closed dressing rooms we had a park-like setting that encouraged the bands to hang out together, play pinball and trade road stories. Bands didn't usually knock on other band's doors, but this way they were thrown together and could enjoy each other's company.

Steven Tyler outside his dressing room RV at World Series of Rock, 1975 ©Janet Macoska

> **The first time a tour manager would meet Wendy, he was looking for her boss. The next time he came to town, he knew she was the boss!** *Jules Belkin*

Wendy Stein backstage with Ted Nugent

Our promoter's rep Wendy Stein was one of the reasons Belkin Productions had an excellent reputation. As one of the first women in the country to do concert production, she fulfilled the band's rider, oversaw show setup, day-of-show production and tear down. Soft-spoken with a big smile, she earned the respect of tour managers of the biggest bands in the world. Wendy worked with Jules for 10 years and left to marry Fred Ordower, who at the time was with Jam Productions in Chicago. At their wedding, Jules walked Wendy down the aisle.

> My pediatrician advised "Get a sitter, Fran. Not a divorce." I jumped at the chance to follow doctor's orders, and ended up working all the outdoor concerts, helping to decorate the backstage dressing room area, and loading my car with fresh flowers for the RVs and catering tent on the day of the show. It was exhilarating to be in the dressing room trailers, just thinking about who would be in them later that day! *Fran Belkin*

The local and touring crews needed to be fed starting on day one of the build up, so the catering tent was one of the first priorities. Our production staff and the staging crew arrived four to five days in advance to build the show: erect the scaffolding, distribute the power, lay the field tarps, hang the lights, and create the dressing room world. Three meals a day were catered, along with beverage service all day. When the productions became more sophisticated, crews worked 24 hours a day to get everything set. Now a fourth meal had to be served in the middle of the night.

Agora owner Hank LoConti stops by the catering tent to visit Fran and Maryellen, 1974

  " For the first show, Jules rented a large grill and ordered hot dogs with all the sides. I pitched in and made a huge pot of chili to put on the dogs, carved a giant watermelon and filled it with fruit. I brought my babysitter, Maryellen, (who somehow got hold of a chef's hat) to the stadium and we served dinner to the entire crew and band members. It was great fun, but tons of work. After that show, Jules decided to hire Paul Hom, the smartest decision ever. **"** *Fran Belkin*

Wok on!

Paul Hom, the Chinese chef, was an instant hit.

The bands on tour were getting the same food everywhere: fried chicken, deli trays, and hot dogs. So the fresh, delicious food coming out of Paul's huge wok was a real treat. He made fabulous stir fry, cha sui dumplings, succulent barbecued pork, baby bok choy and seasonal vegetables. Paul and his wok were usually set up outside the catering tent. As the smells of stir fry spread, the crew would line up waiting to be served. For the Rolling Stones show, the rain forced Paul and his wok under the stage, wedged in between the scaffolding. The location didn't matter, the lines still formed. Thanks to Paul, Cleveland and the Belkins became known for the greatest food on the road.

The bands' riders started showing up with a clause requiring the "Chinese chef" for their catering!

"Steven Tyler loved fresh squeezed orange juice and sliced turkey, but he wanted proof it was real and not processed. So the rider required that we roast a whole turkey, carve off the white meat, and leave the carcass on the table. There was no fresh-squeezed OJ in the stores back then, so I bought an electric juicer and carried it to all the Aerosmith shows." *Wendy Stein*

"The bands' riders were their road bibles. There was no veering off course. And the English bands' riders were always a little different from the American bands. Rod Stewart specified 'NO AMERICAN BEER' and asked for something called Pimm's No. 1, which our people had never heard of. We finally tracked down the English fruit-based liqueur which you mix with soda or ginger ale to make Pimm's Cup." *Debbie Schaefer, Belkin runner*

Backstage at World Series of Rock, c. 1975. The two side-by-side trailers nearest the stage housed the on-site production offices. One trailer for the band and one for the promoter.

"One band wanted organic dog food. *In Cleveland?* We had never heard of such a thing." *Clayton Townsend, runner*

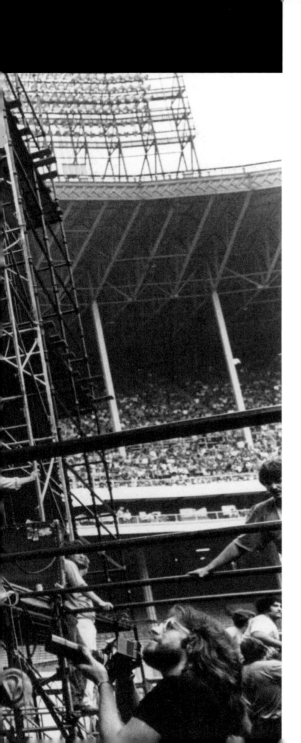

What was the coolest job in town?

Working security at rock concerts, of course! The guys looked tough, wore cool t-shirts, and some even got to hang out backstage. And they got paid!

In the early days, three guys approached Jules and offered to handle show security. Since he didn't have any other options, Sunrise Security was it. They assembled a burly team to work the concerts. Jules asked that the guys who worked out front be trained to interact respectfully with the audience members and handle disruptions so they didn't escalate. The backstage team needed to be helpful and discreet, and never— ever—ask for an autograph.

Working backstage was *the* goal of every security guard, and only the best were privileged to work there, guarding the performers' dressing rooms and escorting them to the stage. Some even got hired as personal security and went on tour with the bands. It was rumored they came to work with a packed suitcase in their car hoping they'd get tapped to go on the road.

Right: Sunrise Security, 1979, Michael Cohen, Jim Singleton, Greg Wagner. Our son Steve (back center) worked with the guys for several summers. Eventually, Hall Entertainment Security (founded by Sunrise employees Jim Singleton and Danny Waits) took over our security needs. Four decades later, they're still keeping concert-goers safe.

> " We approached Jules and offered to handle security "in house" until we passed a state test and formed a company. Luckily, he said yes. "
> *Jim Singleton*

37

Keith Richards, The Rolling Stones, World Series of Rock, Cleveland Stadium, July 1, 1978 ©Janet Macoska

Eighty two-five ain't no jive!

Ladies & Gentlemen: The Rolling Stones

Mick Jagger often wore football jerseys on stage, so Mike and Jules thought a jersey was a natural for their sold-out stadium show. Brian Chalmers from Scene designed the art. The shirt knocked it out of the park, and everyone in the crew loved and wore it.

Eighty Two-Five Ain't No Jive!

SOLD OUT!
82,500 PEOPLE CLEVELAND STADIUM

EMPIRE & Belkin
WELCOME

THE ROLLING STONES

KANSAS
PETER TOSH

Rolling Stones manager Peter Rudge chats with Wendy Stein and Jules in the production trailer at World Series of Rock. Peter and Jules enjoyed a long history with The Who and the Stones. Peter was originally managing The Who when Pete Townshend recommended him to Mick Jagger. As Peter spent more time with the Stones, Townshend got ticked off and changed managers.

Who's the greatest rock 'n' roll band in the world?

"The question flashed in five-foot letters on the scoreboard at the World Series of Rock in the Stadium yesterday afternoon.

But the 82,500 fans—the largest number ever to attend a Cleveland rock concert—didn't have to have the answer flashed."

—Jane Scott, Rock Critic
  The Plain Dealer, July 2, 1978

Critic Jane Scott and Bruno Bornino (her counterpart at The Cleveland Press) at World Series of Rock

" I remember my mom bringing Steve and me down to the World Series of Rock. We were standing on the huge tarps that had been rolled up and stored next to the stage so we could look out at the audience getting drunk and stoned and passing out. Then she would walk us over to the Free Clinic tent. That was her version of anti-drug education **"** *Jamie Belkin, daughter of Fran & Jules*

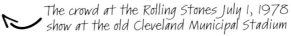

The crowd at the Rolling Stones July 1, 1978 show at the old Cleveland Municipal Stadium

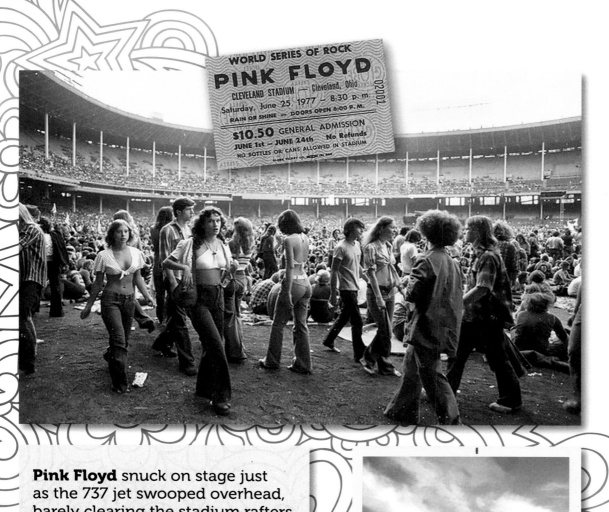

WORLD SERIES OF ROCK
PINK FLOYD
CLEVELAND STADIUM — Cleveland, Ohio
Saturday, June 25, 1977 — 8:30 p.m.
RAIN OR SHINE — DOORS OPEN 6:00 P.M.
$10.50 GENERAL ADMISSION
JUNE 1st — JUNE 24th   No Refunds
NO BOTTLES OR CANS ALLOWED IN STADIUM
02001

Pink Floyd snuck on stage just as the 737 jet swooped overhead, barely clearing the stadium rafters, at a deafening decibel level.

It got everyone's attention, and the band launched into the first notes of *Sheep*. The stunt intentionally scared (and unintentionally sobered up) the crowd. Their manager later told us the band's plane was sitting idle at Burke Lakefront Airport, "So why not put it to good use?" (Pink Floyd was fined $1,500 for violating FAA regulations.)

A band as big as Pink Floyd didn't need an opener.

Pink Floyd was the only World Series show to feature a single band, and Jules wanted to do something very special for the guys. He found a soft leather travel bag—elegant but casual. He ordered six, embossed in gold lettering: one for every band member, and one each for Mike and himself. For the crew, he ordered screenprinted canvas bags.

In 1985, Roger Waters left the band and starting touring solo. From then on, every time he played Cleveland, he would tell Jules that the bag was still his favorite swag. In the early 2000s, he mentioned to Jules that he'd fixed the handle twice, but the bag had finally fallen apart. Jules said, "Hang on. I'll be right back." He hopped in the car, raced home and got his own little-used leather bag. When he handed it to Roger, Roger was thrilled. (This author, on the other hand, was not thrilled. She didn't have the leather bag to photograph for this book.)

" The canvas bags were much bulkier than a normal box of t-shirts, so instead of lugging them to the stadium I decided to take the bags to the band's hotel. I kidnapped a bellboy and convinced him to load the bags onto a luggage cart and use his master key to open every crew member's door so I could place the bags on their beds. Imagine doing that today. **"** *Wendy Stein*

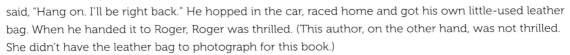

Fleetwood Mac Attack

Stevie Nicks with Jules

The third concert of the '78 series featuring Fleetwood Mac, originally scheduled for August 5, had to be canceled at the last minute due to an injury suffered by Lindsey Buckingham. The rest of the band, Mick Fleetwood, John McVie, Christine McVie and Stevie Nicks, flew to Cleveland to hold a press conference to explain the cancellation.

When the show finally played on August 26, our son Steve was handling important tasks such as handing out sandwiches to the security guards around the stadium. A golf cart was a necessity. When it came time for the band to go on stage, each band member needed a driver with a golf cart to transport them from the dressing room area to the stage steps. Clayton Townsend, one of our runners, was told to drive Christine McVie. He was very unhappy because young Steve Belkin got the desired assignment...driving Stevie Nicks.

Part of Clayton's job as a runner was to buy alcohol and a few cases of wine (the band preferred Blue Nun) for the dressing rooms. None of us ever bothered to ask him how old he was, and we later found out he was only 19. But lucky for him (and us) he had a friend who worked at the County Clerk's office who arranged a fake ID. Problem solved...Clayton shopped freely and "somewhat" legally.

In 1978 and again in 1980, Fleetwood Mac donated Humboldt penguins to the Cleveland Zoo.

Jules (far left) with Fleetwood Mac at the 1978 press conference, which was broadcast live on WMMS

IN CONCERT
FLEETWOOD MAC

SPECIAL GUESTS
GEILS
BOB WELCH
EDDIE MONEY

SAT., AUGUST 5 - 4:00 P.M.
CLEVELAND LAKEFRONT STADIUM

John Courage was Fleetwood Mac's long-time road manager. Stevie Nicks nicknamed him "Sister Golden Hair".

John Courage & Jules Embracing after settlement of Fleetwood Mac show- " Were in the Money"

IT'S ANOTHER
FLEETWOOD MAC attack!
CLEVELAND

"Holy rock'n'roll! I still get emails from people wanting the Fleetwood Mac Attack shirt. It's even sought after by fans in Australia. If the band ever licensed it, it would sell like crazy down under."

David Helton

THE JOHN CARROLL STUDENT UNIO[N]
in cooperation with
WMMS RADIO—PRESENTS IN PER[SON]

MOTT [THE]
HOOP[LE]

★ SPECIAL GUEST: AEROSMITH

SAT., OCT. 13th–8 P.M.
JOHN CARROLL GYMNASIUM
TICKETS $5 ADVANCE $6 DOOR   ALL SEATS RESERVED

TICKETS ON SALE NOW: JOHN CARROLL GYM BOX OFFICE, ALL
CLEVELAND TUX SHOPS, WARD'S FOLLY, SARTORIUM AND
PUBLIC HALL BOX OFFICE.

A BELKIN PRODUCTION

WELCOME
1979
WORLD SERIES of ROCK   GAME #1
AEROSMITH-TED NUGENT
ALSO STARRING
JOURNEY
THIN LIZZY
AC/DC
SAT., JULY 28, 1979
CLEVELAND LAKEFRONT STADIUM

Aerosmith:
From opening act to
headlining the World Series

The first time Jules booked Aerosmith in '73, they were the opening act for the Mahavishnu Orchestra at Case Western Reserve University.

Mahavishnu was late getting to the gig and there was no time for the opening act to play without pushing the show past the noise curfew. Jules asked Aerosmith not to play and he would pay them anyhow....they were shocked. Promoters didn't pay *not* to play! Six months later, Aerosmith returned to open for Mott the Hoople. They remembered Jules this time. Over the next 30 years, Belkin would promote over 75 Aerosmith shows around the country.

Jules, Aerosmith singer Steven Tyler, and band manager David Krebs, World Series of Rock 1979

By 1976, Aerosmith was one of the biggest bands in the world and was booked to headline World Series of Rock. Stadium officials refused to allow seating on the field to prevent damage to the new turf, and Aerosmith refused to play without fans on the field. The show was canceled.

Aerosmith was even bigger the next year, but canceled again after band member Joe Perry was injured at a previous concert. Jules decided that opener Todd Rundgren was so popular at the moment that he could headline the show. And Jules was right.

Todd Rundgren's Utopia was moved up the bill, with Ted Nugent, Southside Johnny and the Asbury Jukes, and last minute addition Nazareth. Even without Aerosmith, the show had the largest "day of show" ticket sales in the history of World Series of Rock.

Aerosmith would eventually get their chance to headline a sold out 1979 World Series of Rock show, supported by Ted Nugent, Journey, and Thin Lizzy. It was an historic show, as Joe Perry quit the band after this concert.

Pat Marrow - Journey

Thankfully, Wendy Stein (center) often had a Polaroid camera to capture backstage moments with the bands.

❝ Some of Todd Rundgren's equipment and instruments disappeared from Music Hall overnight between his two shows—under the not-so-watchful eye of a security guard. The following morning, we received the ransom call: *'If you ever want to see the gear again, deliver ONE HUNDRED DOLLARS to a phone booth on Payne Avenue.'* That was a lot of money in 1974. I got the cash, nervously dropped it off, and was sweating bullets as I ran back to my car. Todd never saw the equipment again. **❞** *Wendy Stein*

Jules at the World Series of Rock, July 15, 1978

The Drop

Every show had a *drop*: the ticket stubs that could be hand counted, if needed, to audit the show attendance. The deal between Belkin Productions and Art Modell (who owned the Browns and operated the stadium) was that after the World Series of Rock concerts, Modell's people would count the drop and he would be paid based on the number of stubs.

After one of the early concerts, Modell told Jules there were 73,000 ticket stubs. Jules said, "That's impossible. There were only 71,000 tickets sold." Jules decided to look through the drop, and he found over 2,000 counterfeit tickets.

This soon became a major problem for every promoter in the country. Creative counterfeiting was rampant, and easily fooled the busy ticket takers at the gate.

Cleveland had the World Series. Meanwhile, Buffalo rocked with Summerfest at the Stadium.

Beginning in 1974, Jules produced major shows at Rich Stadium in Buffalo, NY in partnership with Festival East. Many of the concerts mirrored the World Series of Rock lineups.

> **"** I remember spending much of my summers in Buffalo. We'd arrive three to four days before each show for setup. Looking back, I wonder who took care of our kids during all those years. **"** *Fran Belkin*

SUMMERFEST AT RICH STADIUM

7/6/74 Eric Clapton • The Band **7/26/74** Emerson, Lake & Palmer • James Gang • Lynyrd Skynyrd **8/11/74** Crosby, Stills, Nash & Young • Santana • Jessie Colin Young **8/25/74** Chicago • The Doobie Brothers • Ozark Mountain Daredevils **7/12/75** Yes • Johnny Winter • Ace • J. Geils Band **7/20/75** The Eagles • Seals & Crofts • Judy Collins • Dan Fogelberg **8/8/75** The Rolling Stones • Bobby Womack • The Outlaws **7/10/76** Peter Frampton • Johnny & Edgar Winter • Todd Rundgren **8/7/76** Elton John • Boz Scaggs • John Miles **6/19/77** Blue Oyster Cult • Lynyrd Skynyrd • Ted Nugent **8/20/77** Yes • Bob Seger • J. Geils Band • Donavan **7/4/78** Rolling Stones • Journey • Atlanta Rhythm Section • April Wine **7/28/78** Fleetwood Mac • Foreigner • Bob Welch • Pablo Cruise **9/27/81** Rolling Stones • Journey • George Thorogood **7/3/82** Foreigner • Loverboy • Ted Nugent • Iron Maiden **9/26/82** The Who • The Clash • David Johannsen

Top: Fran celebrates a job well done—painting full sheets of plywood for the stage barrier for Summerfest at the Stadium (center photo). Left: Tuxedo jacket swag for the August 20, 1977 Yes concert, partially sponsored by a tuxedo company

Early stadium shows were a free-for-all with general admission for all concertgoers. Reserve seating for stadium shows started in the early '80s.

By the time of the final encore*
in 1980, nearly a million rock fans
had weathered the crowds, the
cancellations, the chaos, and more
than a few Cleveland thunderstorms
to experience some of the greatest
rock concerts of all time:

THE WORLD SERIES OF ROCK

6/23/74	The Beach Boys • Joe Walsh & Barnstorm • Lynyrd Skynrd • REO Speedwagon
8/4/74	Emerson, Lake & Palmer • Climax Blues Band • James Gang
9/1/74	Crosby, Stills, Nash & Young • Santana • The Band • Jesse Colin Young
5/31/75	The Beach Boys • Chicago
6/14/75	The Rolling Stones • Tower of Power • The J. Geils Band • Joe Vitale's Madmen
7/11/75	Yes • Joe Walsh • Michael Stanley Band • Ace
8/23/75	Rod Stewart & Faces • Uriah Heep • Aerosmith • Blue Oyster Cult • Mahogany Rush
6/5/77	Todd Rundgren & Utopia • Ted Nugent • Southside Johnny & the Asbury Jukes • Nazareth
6/25/77	Pink Floyd
8/6/77	Peter Frampton • Bob Seger & the Silver Bullet Band • The J. Geils Band • Derringer
7/1/78	The Rolling Stones • Kansas • Peter Tosh
7/15/78	Electric Light Orchestra • Foreigner • Journey • Trickster
8/26/78	Fleetwood Mac • Bob Welch • The Cars • Todd Rundgren & Utopia • Eddie Money
7/28/79	Aerosmith • Ted Nugent • Journey • Thin Lizzy • AC/DC • Scorpions
7/19/80	Bob Seger & the Silver Bullet Band • The J. Geils Band • Eddie Money • Def Leppard

*The final encore was Bob Seger, singing a rock and roll medley that
 ended, appropriately, with a cover of Chuck Barry's *Let It Rock*.

World Series of Rock cloudburst,
September 1, 1974
©Janet Macoska

Top: Steve Belkin, age 7, wears the first Belkin t-shirt and hangs out with John Entwistle and Pete Townshend. Bottom: Steve sits in the rowboat while Jamie Belkin, age 5, decides whether to join him.

Saturday, June 27th
The WHO
JAMES GANG
Special Guest Star
JAMES TAYLOR
Cleveland Public Hall
$5 Advance — $6 Door
All Seats Reserved
TICKETS ON SALE NOW!

The Hippie Picnic with The Who

The Who had played Cleveland in the late '60s, and returned in June 1970 as the headliner. Mike booked the show and added the James Gang, a band he managed, as the opening act. Opening for The Who was huge, and the James Gang didn't disappoint. The audience was on their feet when they left the stage. Then, James Taylor came out with his acoustic guitar, and the energy was sucked out of the room. When The Who finally took the stage, the crowd exploded in cheers. This show is recognized in the annals of rock and roll as one of the worst concert lineups in history.

The Who had the day off after the show, and Mike wanted to host a picnic for them. Mike and Jules had small yards, so James Gang drummer Jimmy Fox suggested his fiancée Diane ask her father to use their family farm. Her dad initially didn't want a "bunch of long-haired hippies" on his property, but he relented. Eventually, he even came outside and started talking to Pete Townshend and the others. Later, he commented how surprised he was to meet such intelligent, informed, terrific people.

The first Belkin t-shirt, 1970

The Who, Richfield Coliseum, December 9, 1975 ©Janet Macoska

"The band is freezing! Turn up the heat!"

The Who's people kept demanding it, but that wasn't even a possibility the night the band played the Pontiac Silverdome. The new stadium was basically an outdoor venue, but with a huge Teflon fabric cover to protect it from the severe elements. It wasn't possible for it to be heated like an arena, and a December concert was an iffy proposition.

Doing the first big rock show at the Silverdome was a major compliment to Belkin Productions Detroit (see page 69). The paint was still fresh when 76,000 people attended the inaugural concert in 1975.

james
gang
miami

james
gang
BANG

Out all night,
sleep all day.
I know what
you're doing.

lyrics from Funk #49

Dale Peters, Joe Walsh, and Jimmy Fox in an early James Gang publicity shot.

james gang

In '69, Mike began managing James Gang, a Cleveland-area rock band. He had shirts printed, and at the end of the show the band would throw them out into the audience to the frenzy of fans. The lucky ones who got shirts wore them all the time and gave the band free publicity. Mike was one of the first managers who realized the importance of t-shirts as marketing tools.

The James Gang enjoyed great popularity while touring with The Who. Their huge 1970 hit, *Funk #49*, was on Billboard's Hot 100 chart for 10 weeks. They had three other top 100 records: *Walk Away, Midnight Man* and *Must Be Love*. After Joe Walsh left the band in 1971, James Gang continued playing and recording but never again achieved chart success. In 1996, the band rallied the hometown crowd at Bill Clinton's final campaign rally before his re-election as president.

❝We met the James Gang in Cleveland. We played with them and we loved them all straight away...Mike Belkin had this big barbecue on a sunny day. It was just absolutely wonderful. ❞
Pete Townshend, in 2006 recalling the 1970 picnic

Wild Cherry's only hit single went number one in 1976, but over 40 years later *Play That Funky Music* remains on Billboard's list of the All-Time Top 100 Songs.

Not bad for a tune that started as a scribble with a borrowed pen on a bartender's order pad after a fan shouted, *"Are you white boys gonna play some funky music?"* After recording the song, studio engineer Ken Hamann brought it to the attention of Sweet City Records. Mike Belkin and Carl Maduri signed them. *Play That Funky Music* wound up their only hit—with a pair of Grammy nominations for Best R&B Album and Best New Artist. In 1979, they "dis-banded."

Ten years later, rapper Vanilla Ice released a version of *Play That Funky Music*, without crediting Bobby Parissi for songwriting. Based on the single, Ice was signed to a record deal. Eventually, Bobby sued and won 85% of everything Vanilla Ice made on the song. Later, MTV asked Bobby if he hated Vanilla Ice. The reply: ***"No. I want to adopt him!"***

Wild Cherry band and management, c. 1977. Front row: Bobby Parissi (lead singer), Mark Avsec (keyboards), Joey Porello, Unknown, Jules, Back Row: Chris Maduri, Brian Bassett, (guitar), Ronnie Beitle (drums), Unknown, Mike, Carl Maduri

> **❝** They didn't have a name and had to pick one because they were about to record their first album. Bobby Parissi was recuperating after a hospital stay and the band members came to visit him and come up with a name. Bobby looked over at his nightstand, noticed the box of cough drops, and his face lit up. "That's it!" he said. "We'll call the band Wild Cherry." And so it was. **❞** *Mark Avsec*

Jules and Fran arrive at the 1977 Grammy Awards, where Wild Cherry was nominated for Best New Artist. (Starland Vocal Band would win... but when's the last time anybody got down to *Afternoon Delight*?)

Wild Cherry Promotional T-Shirt 1976-1977

Baby what you gonna do when the fire is through
And you find he's out looking for somebody new
Cause you did everything that he wanted you to do
And now you're all alone and crying...

lyrics from Lover

Hometown Hero World-Class Talent: Michael Stanley

Nothing captures the Cleveland rock and roll experience like an MSB concert. If you grew up here in the '70s and '80s, you most likely were part of the record-setting attendance at the Coliseum in 1979, '81 and '82 (and at one of the *four* sold out shows at Blossom Music Center in '82). Michael wrote song after song, illuminating our feelings and deepest fears, telling us what love is and what love isn't, opening our eyes to the transient world of rock bands, the loneliness of being on the road. Michael is a poet who reaches deep into our psyche to explain what we're feeling. Michael Stanley continues to play, Mike Belkin still manages him, and fans still sing along to every word. Michael Stanley remains one of Cleveland's favorite sons.

> **"** One night Michael Stanley came to our house and, perched on a high stool with his guitar, sang songs and told stories of his days on the road, some funny, some poignant. Everyone in the room agreed that it was a "pinch me" moment—a rare opportunity to glimpse into the mind of a great songwriter. And why was he here? Performing a fundraiser for the Cleveland International Film Festival as a favor to me. **"** *Jules Belkin*

Michael Stanley Band, Richfield Coliseum, 1981 ©Janet Macoska

Legendary Legend Valley

Legend Valley was originally a farm located near Newark, Ohio (the locals pronounce it Nerk, Ahia), where friends and family of the owners gathered to jam to their love of music. Hank Lo Conti, owner of Cleveland's Agora Theatre & Ballroom, was aware of this awesome place and approached Jules with the opportunity to develop it for outdoor concerts together. The big open field with a natural bowl surrounded by grassy, gently sloping hillsides was the perfect place to set a stage. The surrounding farms were available for parking lots, so everyone could profit. Legend Valley was a concert lover's paradise: music royalty, thousands of fans, and coolers were allowed *and* encouraged. The party atmosphere in the parking lots sometimes started days before the show, especially when the Grateful Dead played. Hank and Jules promoted shows there for years: Alabama, Ted Nugent, Heart, Charlie Daniels Band, Willie Nelson, and countless others—precursors to festivals like Bonaroo, Coachella and Lollapalooza.

(But Legend Valley wasn't paradise for all. There were never enough security guards to adequately protect the perimeter. Kids were constantly trying to jump the fence. Belkin production staffer Brian Hansen once summed it up memorably: "I'd like to fill a hose with black ink and stinky sulfur and spray all the jumpers!)

From 1986 to 2003, the venue was renamed Buckeye Lake Music Center, but most of us never stopped calling it Legend Valley.

Stacey Harper is one of the top promoter reps in the industry. She came to Belkin Productions right after graduating from Kent State University in 1976 where she worked on the college concert board. Stacey began working under Wendy but quickly mastered her skills and began to produce large arena and stadium shows, including Legend Valley. Stacey continues to work with Live Nation, and all the veteran touring production managers know her and love to work with her.

" If Belkin is ever willing to let Stacey go, let me know— we want her. " *Robbie Taylor, Grateful Dead Road Manager*

UP IN FLAMES!

Todd Rundgren was still performing on stage, and it was close to the end of the show when Jules noticed a fire up near the entrance area. He went to investigate. It had rained the day before so the crew had put down straw on the muddy ground next to the wooden entrance hut. Someone must have tossed down a lit match or cigarette and the straw caught fire and burned down the entrance, In the meantime, Eric Gardner, Rundgren's manager, had been questioning Jules about the audience count. Eric decided to sue claiming that Jules had burned the evidence of the drop that was in the entrance hut.

The lawsuit went to arbitration, and the arbitrator was from the musician's union, which didn't bode well for Jules. Eric said he could see from the stage that our people were setting fire to the entrance. Jules countered with photos showing that you couldn't possibly see the entrance from the stage. Then Eric claimed Jules had destroyed the drop on purpose. Jules was prepared. He brought out a black garbage bag and dumped all the tickets on the table. Every ticket was accounted for. And Eric left a loser.

JULY 15, 1979

Legend Valley

THE FIRST
LEGEND VALLEY
ROCK & ROLL SHOW

> Legend has it that Alice Cooper was the first to deface the wall with his signature, and from then on every band that played the Coliseum added their own. From afar, the 40-foot wall across from the dressing rooms could have been overlooked as graffiti, but up close it was a living history of Cleveland rock and roll. *Steve Belkin*

BELKIN PRODUCTIONS BY ARRANGE

AN EVENING WITH

ERIC CLAPTON

AND HIS BAND

TUESDAY APRIL 1

RICHFIE COLISE

ALL SEATS RESER
TICKETS AVAILABLE AT THE COL
AND ALL TICKETRON L
TO CHARGE BY PHONE
524-0000 OR TOLL-FREE

ERIC CLAPTON APPEARS PROMPTLY AT 7:30

Budweiser

WMMS / MTV / BELKIN PRODUCTIONS PRESENT

THE POLICE

...eld, Cleveland, OH

...aturday 8:00 P.M.

...TRON outlets and the Coliseum box office

The Coliseum

"THE PALACE ON THE PRAIRIE"

Photos: Foghat Guitar Duel, 1976; Madonna, 1987 ©Janet Macoska

Fun while it lasted...

20 memory-packed years at Richfield Coliseum

The 20,000-seat Richfield Coliseum opened in 1974, replacing Cleveland Public Hall as the region's primary indoor concert venue. The location in northern Summit County was "ideally situated within a one-hour drive for nearly five million sports and music fans," owner Nick Mileti said at the time.

Frank Sinatra entertained on opening night, and two nights later Stevie Wonder headlined the first pop concert. Then, for the next 20 years fans braved white-knuckle winter driving, one-lane highway exit ramps and rural access roads to make it to the Coliseum by show time.

Finally in 1990, Cuyahoga County voters approved a sin tax to lure the teams and concerts back to Cleveland. Gund Arena (now called Quicken Loans Arena) opened downtown in 1994 with Billy Joel.

After hundreds of Belkin-produced shows in Richfield, the Coliseum was shuttered. The *Palace on the Prairie* sat vacant for several years until then owners, the Gund family, decided to work with the Trust for Public Land to reclaim the property and transfer it to the Cuyahoga Valley National Park. Now, the only music heard at the old Coliseum site are the songs of birds.

Won't Get Used Again

The team from *Belkin Productions* waves goodbye to the *Richfield Coliseum* after *Roger Daltrey* played the last show at the Cleveland-area venue September 1st. Richfield is being replaced by the new *Gateway Arena* which is scheduled to open October 17th with Billy Joel. Pictured (L-R) *Michael Belkin, Barry Gabel, Chris Risner, Jules Belkin, Fran Belkin, Dan Kemer, Stacey Harper* and *Jamie Belkin-Opalich*.

Michael Belkin, Mike's son, had finished college and under Jules was learning the booking aspect of the business. He worked production first and then started booking clubs and colleges. Jules encouraged him to build relationships with the young, new agents who were managing the up-and-coming bands. He gradually took over more of the booking and today he is a respected promoter. Michael now heads up the regional Live Nation office, still housed in the former Belkin Productions' Chagrin Falls building.

Bruuuce!

On August 10, 1975, Bruce Springsteen and the E Street Band played to a sold out Allen Theatre in Playhouse Square. Ever since, northeast Ohio and Bruce have had a love affair—Bruce loved playing here and the fans adored him. The New Year's Eve 1978 show was Bruce's gift to Cleveland: he scheduled his entire tour around playing Cleveland that night and again New Year's Day.

We made this hoodie to show our gratitude for all the dates Jules had been given, and listed them on the back of the shirt to tell the rest of the world.

73,500 ECSTATIC FANS SAW

BELKIN AND THE "BOSS"

ON TOUR WITH

BRUCE SPRINGSTEEN & THE E STREET BAND

1978

TOLEDO JUNE, 5	6,000	LANSING NOV. 18	6,000
CLEVELAND, AUG. 30	14,000	DETROIT	
DETROIT		COBO DEC. 30	11,000
MASONIC SEPT. 2	4,500	CLEVELAND DEC. 31,	
COLUMBUS SEPT. 5	4,000	JAN. 1	28,000

COMPLETELY SOLD OUT!

"One of the sound guys had been giving Stacey a pain all day, complaining about everything, and was just generally miserable. At midnight, Tom Einhouse and I were stationed in the rafters to drop confetti down onto the audience. Stacey gave us a few extra packages to drop onto the sound board to wish this guy a Happy New Year. In the wee hours, we saw him with a vacuum cleaner still trying to get all the confetti out of his sound board."
Clayton Townsend, runner

"New Year's Eve was a great show—everyone was in a celebratory mood—and the Coliseum hosted a party for the band and their staff in the owner's suite. Everyone was at the party but Bruce, he stayed down in the dressing room area and received guests until 3 a.m.! There was a long line of people; he spoke to each person. Bruce had endless energy for his fans and was always gracious." *Wendy Stein*

Photo, left page: Bruce Springsteen, Ronnie Spector, and one of The Cleveland Boys (fan club) backstage at Richfield Coliseum, February 17, 1977 ©Janet Macoska

The night Bruce blanked on Born to Run.

The River Tour kicked off on October 3, 1980 with Belkin Productions at Ann Arbor's Crisler Arena. In rehearsal, Wendy noticed Bruce struggling to remember the words to *Born to Run*, so she sent one of the college kids to his dorm to get the album with the lyrics printed on the liner.

That night, he opened the show with the song—and again drew a blank. This time, the audience helped out.

"I was so nervous I forgot all the words," Bruce later recalled.

Later that week, he played back-to-back dates at Richfield Coliseum, followed by two nights in Detroit. Then, the band set off on a world tour totaling over 115 dates. Nearly a year later, Bruce and the band returned to The Coliseum for the homecoming leg. They played two steamy July nights in Richfield and then two more in Detroit.

The excitement at Bruce's sold out shows was palpable and the tour was a huge success, but my memorable moment was finally learning that Bruce hated to be called "The Boss." Our custom embroidered shirt probably didn't impress.

> I left Belkin Productions in 1981 to work for Paul Simon on his film, *One Trick Pony*, which was being shot in Cleveland. One day I was driving Paul to a dentist appointment, and Springsteen was playing on the radio.
>
> 'Do you really like Springsteen?' Paul asked me, perplexed that anyone could be a fan. 'This guy is going nowhere. He only sings about old cars and other depressing stuff.' *Clayton Townsend*

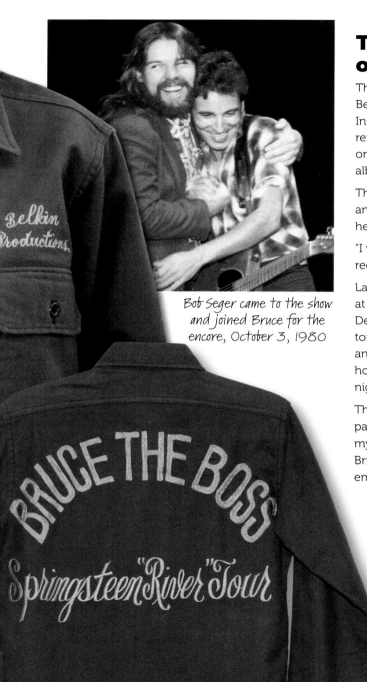

Bob Seger came to the show and joined Bruce for the encore, October 3, 1980

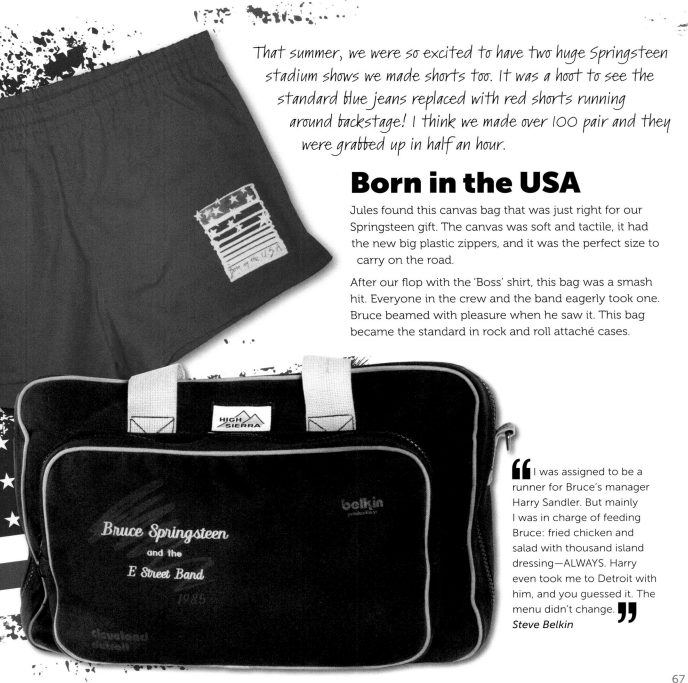

That summer, we were so excited to have two huge Springsteen stadium shows we made shorts too. It was a hoot to see the standard blue jeans replaced with red shorts running around backstage! I think we made over 100 pair and they were grabbed up in half an hour.

Born in the USA

Jules found this canvas bag that was just right for our Springsteen gift. The canvas was soft and tactile, it had the new big plastic zippers, and it was the perfect size to carry on the road.

After our flop with the 'Boss' shirt, this bag was a smash hit. Everyone in the crew and the band eagerly took one. Bruce beamed with pleasure when he saw it. This bag became the standard in rock and roll attaché cases.

"I was assigned to be a runner for Bruce's manager Harry Sandler. But mainly I was in charge of feeding Bruce: fried chicken and salad with thousand island dressing—ALWAYS. Harry even took me to Detroit with him, and you guessed it. The menu didn't change.**"**
Steve Belkin

Bob Seger was from Detroit,

and his Midwestern rock music spoke to the hearts of his fans in Cleveland. Jules had an unusually close relationship with Bob and his manager, Punch Andrews, who was a personal friend for many years. 1980 was Bob Seger's second World Series of Rock, his first as a headliner.

Bob Seger
THE PALACE OF AUBURN HILLS 1986.
BLACKBIRD • BELKIN • CELLAR DOOR

Belkin
PRESENTS
Bob Seger
& the
silver bullet band
SPECIAL GUESTS
MOLLY HATCHET
DECEMBER 20th
TOLEDO SPORTS ARENA
7,500
DECEMBER 22nd & 23rd
RICHFIELD COLISEUM
30,000
SOLD OUT!

1980
World Series of Rock
Cleveland Stadium
July 19
Belkin
PRODUCTIONS

Bob Seger &
The Silver Bullet Band

World Series
of Rock 1980

Definitely No Stranger
In These Towns!

Made in Detroit
Phil Ober and the Belkin Motown Family

Jules and Phil began working together in the late '60s when Jules started booking concerts in Detroit. Every big act that came to Cleveland would also go to Detroit. At first the shows were downtown at Cobo Hall and Joe Louis Arena. Jules and Phil eventually worked together all over Michigan, with Jules booking the concerts and Phil handling advertising and production.

In 1975, the Silverdome (one of the first covered stadiums in the country) made its debut in Detroit. Opening a new building is an important event, and Belkin Productions was invited to produce the first concert: The Who (see page 53). From then on, Belkin Detroit booked the Silverdome almost exclusively. Later, when The Palace of Auburn Hills opened in 1988, it was one of the first upscale, state-of-the-art facilities in the country, and Jules and Phil were fortunate to forge an exclusive booking agreement.

Phil was an important part of our lives and our company. His Michigan shows were a huge source of revenue and pride. Our families are close, celebrating life events together. He was like another brother to Jules.

Clockwise from L: Steve Belkin, Michael Ober, Betsy Delis (Jules' assistant), Phil Ober, Denny Young (marketing, BPI), Marilyn Desjardins (VP of Marketing & Booking, The Palace), Sam Gabel, Jules, Jamie Belkin, Fran, Barry Gabel (VP Marketing, BPI), Joni Ober, Stacey Harper (VP Production, BPI).

Keep playing. The audience loves you!

In March 1971, Geils was opening for Black Sabbath and Mountain at Cleveland Public Hall. It was going to be a long evening—with a curfew—so Jules made clear Geils had only 30 minutes to play. The band wasn't happy, but they went on, and got a great reception.

While they were on stage, Jules received the call that Mountain was delayed by a snowstorm in Philly. He went to the side of the stage and told Geils lead singer Peter Wolf that since the audience loved them, they should play another 30-minute set. The band played their hearts out.

Then Jules got yet another call: Black Sabbath was delayed because guitarist Tommy Iommi had left his artificial fingertip in Buffalo and couldn't play without it. (He lost the real one in an accident at age 17).

Jules went back to the stage. "You're killing it! Play another 30."

While Geils continued to play, Jules tried to find a solution to the bigger problem. Eventually the show was canceled, but Peter Wolf was always grateful for the exposure Jules made possible. J. Geils played in the lineup for many Belkin shows, and Jules and Peter were always eager to catch up.

If your t-shirt doesn't say DD on the sleeve, it's just underwear.

Daffy Dan's t-shirts were the coolest tees in town, and between 1973 and 1978, Dan Grey grew from one location to 27 stores selling just about every imaginable slogan or image heat pressed onto a t-shirt while you waited.

70

1978 Foreigner t-shirt with DD on the sleeve

It's 1977, KISS is a phenomenon and Jules is selling out their shows throughout the Midwest.

KISS' manager Bill Aucoin and agent Wally Meyrowitz are flying high—the money is just rolling in. (Aucoin's deal was 20% of all record, concert and merchandise income.) Jules was doing lots of business with them and they became fast friends.

Bill and Wally decided to take a vacation together in Europe and invited us to come along. I had met Wally one time, but not his wife Laurie, or Bill and his boyfriend. So here I was going on vacation with total strangers. And they were making reservations in five-star hotels, which surprised and concerned us. Jules and I had both been to Europe when we were younger, but it had been "Europe on $5 a Day."

We flew to Paris and the first night we all went to dinner at a swanky restaurant. Bill ordered a $300 bottle of wine. (Jules and I didn't know the first thing about wine.) We ate the great food and drank the excellent wine and toasted KISS many times! Bill picked up the check—we were relieved.

The next night, we went to another well-known restaurant. This time Wally ordered a $200 bottle. Again we ate, drank and toasted KISS. Wally picked up the check.

On the third night, there was no getting around it; it was our turn. Jules asked the sommelier to recommend a good wine. It was about $150 a bottle. Then after dinner, they all ordered a vintage brandy at $50 a glass...and then ordered a second round.

The bill came to over $500. Jules handed the waiter our credit card, which he politely handed back with the words, *"No plastique!"*

We were stunned. I reached into my purse and got our traveler's checks. A few were hundreds, but the rest were twenties. Poor Jules just kept signing and signing checks until he finally had enough to cover the bill.

Bill Aucoin holding a KISS gold record, c.1976. Fran and Jules with Wally Meyrowitz at World Series of Rock 1974

The next morning at breakfast, Jules came clean. He explained to Bill and Wally that he was a lowly promoter—not an agent or a manager—and we couldn't keep up with them or their taste in wine. So we agreed to split the checks, and they split the wine separately.

We left Paris in two rental cars, three of us in each car and drove all over the Loire Valley, visiting vineyards, eating French food and toasting KISS.

One of the blizzards of early 1978 was kicking up outside while KISS was on stage at the Richfield Coliseum. By the end of the show, cars were buried in snow, and kids had to sleep in the concourse until morning.

The band's limousines had been inside the building so they weren't snowed under. The limos got out and we also braved the treacherous roads, eventually getting to a big party at Swingo's Celebrity Hotel in downtown Cleveland. As the night wore on, the roads got worse and worse, so we just checked into Swingo's too.

" We opened our hotel room door to find a round bed and mirrors on the ceiling! No headboard, no reading lamp, and not even a nightstand to put one on.

I turned to Jules and said "How am I going to read?"

"Dear, I don't think this bed was made for reading," Jules said. " *Fran Belkin*

" Our history with KISS encompassed all of its mutations...make-up, no make-up, changing personnel, changing managers, and ultimately, their induction into the Rock & Roll Hall of Fame. I always felt that they were one of the most approachable rock and roll bands. " *Jules Belkin*

WMMS and BELKIN PRODUCTIONS present
KISS
YOU ASKED FOR IT...
YOU GOT it...
SHOUT IT OUT
ALL NEW BIZARRE STAGE SHOW!!!
SPECIAL GUEST: ARTFU
SEE!! ... THE EXPLO
OF THE POW

"New look" two-color sweatshirt for the Setting Heaven and Earth on Fire tour with design by Leo Schleicher, December 14, 1984, Richfield Coliseum.

Photo: Gene Simmons, 1978 ©Janet Macoska

KISS
Setting Heaven on Fire with Belkin Productions!

In the early '80s, Jules got a call from Gene Simmons that KISS was struggling. He asked Jules to take a chance on some smaller markets, promising he wouldn't lose money. Jules booked venues in Lexington, Saginaw, Toledo, Dayton, and the Agora Ballroom in Cleveland. Gene and Paul often credit Belkin Productions with helping to relaunch their career.

The night Jules joined KISS ↰

During the KISS Alive/Worldwide tour, every promoter had to come to the show in full makeup as a member of the band, or pay a $2,500 penalty. Most promoters came as Gene Simmons or Paul Stanley—except Jules. He was the only one to arrive made up as drummer Peter Criss.

KISS tour manager and good friend Paco Zimmer with Jules, July, 1996. The band plays the music, but Paco collects the check.

Left: Hot in the Shade Tour, 1990
Right: Psycho Circus Tour, 1998

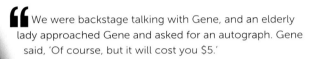

> **"**We were backstage talking with Gene, and an elderly lady approached Gene and asked for an autograph. Gene said, 'Of course, but it will cost you $5.'
>
> She went into her purse, took out $5 and gave it to him and he signed her autograph. We all waited for him to give her the money back, but he just smiled and put the money in his pocket.**"** *Fran Belkin*

In 1982, the band parted ways with manager Bill Aucoin and later hired Doc McGhee, who managed Bon Jovi, Mötley Crüe and other big acts. Doc brought personality and humor to the job of manager; he was fair in his dealings and became a favorite with promoters. KISS has prospered since he took over. We celebrated with Doc when KISS was inducted into the Rock & Roll Hall of Fame in 2014.

> **"**There was a time when each region had a promoter. Some of those guys were terrific and the cream always rises to the top. Jules and his whole family, they were our Cleveland family.**"** *Paul Stanley*

Barry Gabel, Fran, Michael Belkin, Jules and Doc McGhee pose backstage with KISS celebrating the band's 40th anniversary

> **"I was going into the Army in a month (June 1980). I was a member of Belkin Concert Club and I told them it was my last concert. They seated me front row center at a sold out show... Journey and the Babys."** *Concert Club Member*

Bryan Francis Johnson, lead singer, AC/DC, 1986 ©Janet Macoska

ANNOUNCING!! the Belkin CONCERT CLUB

ARE YOU INTERESTED IN?

- The BEST seats to all Belkin Productions Concerts! Belkin Concert Club Members will receive the BEST seats. Members' seats are guaranteed before anyone else can buy them.
- Never having to stand in line or even leave your house to purchase tickets.
- Having advance notice of all Belkin Productions concerts thru your exclusive monthly news letter!
- Receiving a 10% discount on all records and tapes. At Peaches Records & Grapevine Records (Akron). Plus discounts on clothing, official group T-shirts, album cover mirrors and belt buckles. PLUS, other exclusive features available only to Belkin Concert Club members!

Just think — what you save on your purchases through the Belkin's Concert Club will more than pay for your membership!

*Except sale records & tapes.

BELKIN CONCERT CLUB APPLICATION

Yes, standing in line isn't for me! Enroll me now in the Belkin Concert Club! I have read the directions in the next column.

Name _____

Address _____

City _____ Zip _____

Age _____ Phone _____

Education _____ (Most Recent School Attended)

Are You Currently A Student? ☐ Yes ☐ No
                              ☐ Full Time ☐ Part Time

Occupation _____

Belkin CONCERT CLUB

REMEMBER—APPLICATION DEADLINE IS FEB. 1

HERE'S HOW YOU JOIN!!!

Fill out the enclosed form and return with a check or money order for $37.50 made payable to the BELKIN CONCERT CLUB. Enclose a self-addressed stamped envelope and send to:

BELKIN CONCERT CLUB
28001 Chagrin Blvd.
Suite 205
Cleveland, Ohio 44122

Each 1 year membership entitles you to purchase two seats at regular prices by mail to all Belkin Productions concerts in 1979.*(There is a .60 service and handling charge per ticket.) THIS, PLUS ALL THE OTHER EXCLUSIVE CONCERT CLUB FEATURES!

Membership is limited. All applications for membership will be drawn at random by a Certified Public Accountant. Members will be notified of acceptance by Feb. 15. Membership effective March 1, 1979 thru Feb. 29, 1980. Members are automatically eligible for 1980 membership renewal. Deadline for application renewal for those not chosen $37.50 will be returned Feb. 15.

For Further information, call the Belkin Club Hotline — 464-5228.

*Applies only to concerts in the Akron area.

76

"I'm sitting front row center!"

The Belkin Concert Club was the first of its kind in the country.

It was Mike's brainstorm, and the concept was simple. Music fans paid for a membership which gave them early access to concert tickets, they were guaranteed good seats and they didn't have to wait in line. We listed their top three bands on their card so they got the best seats for their favorites.

The $37.50 membership in 1978 would be about $120 in today's dollars—so it was expensive. But the thrill of knowing you would have good seats for any concert was well worth the price. Kids saved up to pay for their membership, and they never scalped their tickets.

The Club grew year after year and it became a large part of the company's revenue. Many promoters around the country followed the Belkin lead and created their own clubs.

And along came our secret weapon...

In 1979, Barry Gabel had graduated from UNC, and was a long-haired musician goofing around in North Carolina. He fell hard for a girl named Sam (a former dancer on the Upbeat TV show) and followed her to Cleveland. Sam's best friend was Michael Stanley's wife, and they got him an interview at Belkin Productions. He was hired the same day: to pick up and open mail in the Concert Club. As soon as he started getting a regular paycheck, Barry and Sam eloped.

In 1981, the job of marketing guy opened up, and Barry jumped at the chance. He was a natural for the job, loved the music, and had a sixth sense for how to promote it. He was also the energy behind promoting the Moscow Circus, Sam Kinison, and Trans Siberian Orchestra. Jules would book these oddball shows and Barry would grab the ball and run with it. Barry's still running the show as Senior Vice President at Live Nation, the successor of Belkin. And he's still falling hard for Sam.

❝ It's actually the only full-time job I've ever had! **❞** *Barry Gabel*

Concert Club
ad 1978

77

Hold onto your hat
Hold onto your heart
Ready, get set
to tear this place apart.
lyrics from Rock! Rock! (till you drop)

Fueled by hits *Photograph, Rock of Ages,* and *Foolin,* Def Leppard was Burning Places to the Ground, and their *Pyromania* album was the catalyst for the 1980s pop-metal movement. Drummer Rick Allen liked this swag shirt so much he wore it for a publicity shot which was subsequently used on the cover of an all-Def Leppard issue of *Metal Mania* magazine. Def Leppard is still touring, and original members of the band signed the cover during a 2018 Cleveland stop.

BELKIN PRODUCTIONS
AND
DEF LEPPARD

BURNING PLACES TO THE GROUND

An unusual shirt with wraparound graphics, printed front and back designed by Leo Schleicher, July 7, 1983

Rolling Stones *Tattoo You* Stadium Tour 1981

Promoter Bill Graham partnered with Belkin Productions and brought The Stones tour to Buffalo's Rich Stadium. At the end of the tour, Bill hosted a sensational party in New Orleans on a paddle boat and invited all the promoters who had worked with him. Everyone was thrilled to have a rare chance to spend time together and to share tour stories.

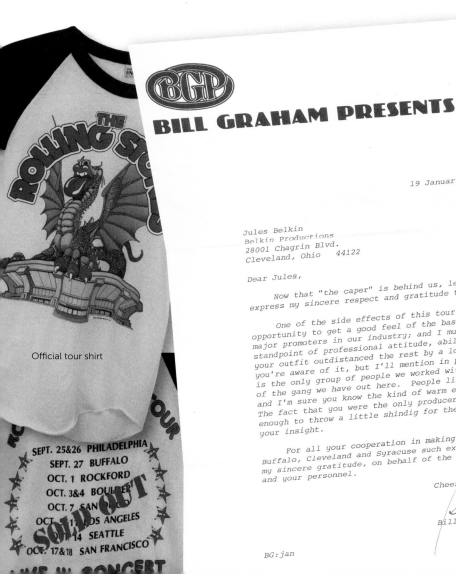

Official tour shirt

SEPT. 25&26 PHILADELPHIA
SEPT. 27 BUFFALO
OCT. 1 ROCKFORD
OCT. 3&4 BOULDER
OCT. 7 SAN
OCT. 11 LOS ANGELES
OCT. 14 SEATTLE
OCT. 17&18 SAN FRANCISCO
SOLD OUT

BGP

BILL GRAHAM PRESENTS

19 January 1982

Jules Belkin
Belkin Productions
28001 Chagrin Blvd.
Cleveland, Ohio   44122

Dear Jules,

Now that "the caper" is behind us, let me take a few moments to express my sincere respect and gratitude to you and your people.

One of the side effects of this tour was that I was given ample opportunity to get a good feel of the basic modus operandi of the major promoters in our industry; and I must say that, from the standpoint of professional attitude, ability and "communal spirit", your outfit outdistanced the rest by a long shot. I'm certain that you're aware of it, but I'll mention in passing anyway that yours is the only group of people we worked with that somewhat reminds me of the gang we have out here. People like Wendy are hard to find, and I'm sure you know the kind of warm effect Fran has in any environment. The fact that you were the only producer on the entire tour who thought enough to throw a little shindig for the traveling crew testifies to your insight.

For all your cooperation in making the Rolling Stones events in Buffalo, Cleveland and Syracuse such excellent productions, I extend my sincere gratitude, on behalf of the entire touring party, to you and your personnel.

Cheers:

Bill Graham

BG:jan

Bill was the man—the premier promoter—and head and shoulders above all the others. He produced the shows at San Francisco's Fillmore and helped launch Grateful Dead, Jefferson Airplane, and Janis Joplin. His relationships were with the bands themselves, not just the agents. When he took a tour around the country, he worked with the local promoters, because they knew their markets. We started in the business at the same time, and I always enjoyed working with Bill. *Jules Belkin*

BELKIN PRODUCTIONS CLEVELAND 1981

LOWER 144 F 1 SEC ROW SEAT

ADMIT ONE THIS DATE ONLY

BELKIN PRODUCTIONS
★★★ PRESENTS ★★★
Rolling Stones
A JOVAN PRESENTATION
RICHFIELD COLISEUM

NOV 17 1981 RICHFIELD, OHIO
TUESDAY 8:00 P.M.

NO REFUND NO EXCHANGE PRICE $15.00

LOWER 144 SEC ROW SEAT

US TOUR 81

After the stadium tour ended, the Stones came to Cleveland for the arena tour, playing the Coliseum on November 16-17, 1981. Stacey and Wendy brainstormed with Jules for some really special swag. The Lacoste shirt was the hottest shirt around and we loved the idea of the famous alligator with a Rolling Stones tongue, but we all agreed it would be too expensive. Instead, Jules bought 100 Le Tigre brand shirts and I spent two days with a razor blade carefully removing the little tiger logos so Brian Fenderbosch at the Scene could screenprint them with the new artwork.

The Stones people went crazy for it and it was worth all the effort. They said it was the most original concept for swag they had been given.

IT'S NOT HARD TO SELL OUT!
THE
WHO
82
BELKIN PRODUCTIONS
CLEVELAND

From left: Sharon Polimeros, Terri Nemeth, Susan Haffey, Betsy Delis, Wendy Stein, Patti Del Villan, Martha Neary, Fran

Wendy Stein, Fran, Bonnie LoConti: Three French Maids ready to please The Who

" For years after that show, the guys from Showco, the sound company, would came back to Cleveland with other bands wearing this shirt from the It's Hard tour. " *Wendy Stein*

The Who, Richfield Coliseum, 1979 ©Janet Macoska

The French Maids say "Who la la!"

If a band had shows two consecutive nights, and it was a band we had a relationship with, we would throw a party the first night after the show. But the night of The Who party was special.

Their tour manager told Wendy to do something out of the ordinary—maybe a costume party. So Wendy rented these authentic French Maid costumes for all the girls in our office and tuxes for the men.

The party was at the Peninsula Nite Club, just a few miles from the Richfield Coliseum, and when the Englishmen in the band and crew walked into the party, they howled with joy at our costumes. What a party—snowing outside, warm inside with good food, lots to drink and everyone dancing with the French maids! Pete and Roger both thanked Jules and Wendy the next day. They said it was their favorite party on the road.

Phil and his band (The Hot Tub Club)

were playing two sold out nights at the Coliseum. After the show, we planned a late night bowling party for the band and their crew, complete with personalized bowling shirts. Unbeknownst to us, tossing a ball down a lane wasn't a popular sport in England. There, they bowled on lawns. Phil didn't have a clue what a gutter ball was, or why we wore the odd shirts, but he caught on quickly and had a blast. During a tour, it's not often a band gets to do something unexpected like bowling.

Original art for the entry passes to the bowling party, by Leo Schleicher

Phil and Fran show off their custom bowling shirts and the sheet cake, June 25, 1985

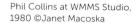

" In '83, we turned the title track from Genesis's new album, *Mama*, into the catchy "A Mama of a Tour." But we should have paid closer attention to what the English rock bands were wearing at the moment. It sure wasn't turquoise new wave-style vests. The guys thanked us, but it was obvious these vests would never be worn. **"**
Fran Belkin

Phil Collins at WMMS Studio, 1980 ©Janet Macoska

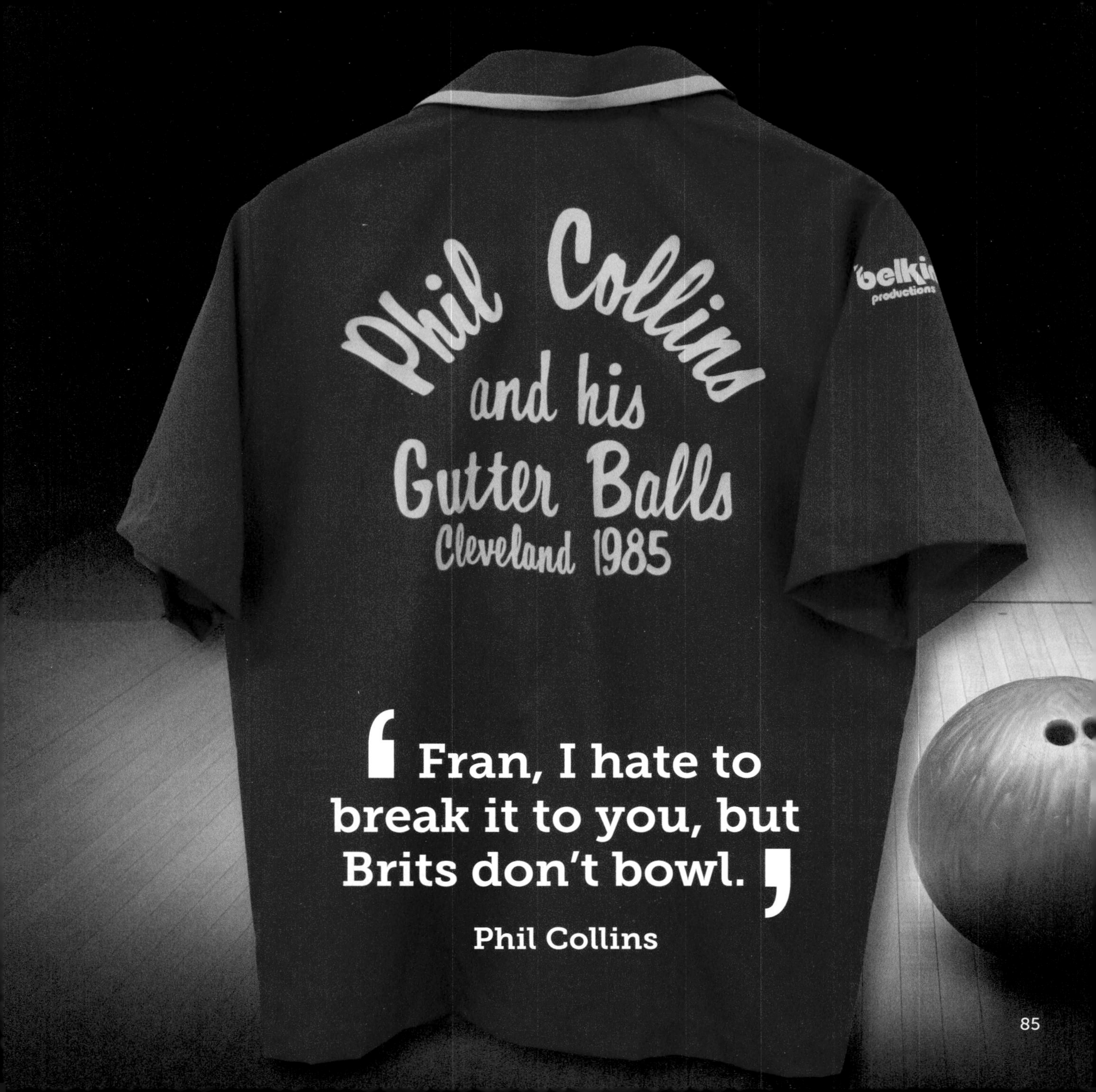

Phil Collins
and his
Gutter Balls
Cleveland 1985

belkin
productions

‘ Fran, I hate to
break it to you, but
Brits don't bowl. ’

Phil Collins

Genesis in 1974 with manager Tony Smith (far left), who became a good friend. Tony also managed Phil Collins' solo career. Genesis first played Cleveland in 1973, and our relationship with Phil and the team continued for over 30 years, including the time in 1985 when Phil surprised Jules with this platinum album, complete with self-portrait.

to
Jules Belkin
thanks for being fabulous,
simply fabulous!
the Hot Tub Club '85

luv
Phil

PLATINUM SALES AWARD

PRESENTED TO
JULES BELKIN
TO COMMEMORATE THE SALE OF MORE THAN
1,000,000 COPIES OF THE
ATLANTIC RECORDS
ALBUM AND CASSETTE
"NO JACKET REQUIRED"

In 1987, Phil was back.

We had already taken him bowling, so this time we took the band and crew to Whirly Ball (a combination of bumper cars and basketball).

Phil didn't want to do Whirly Ball, but I begged him to give it a try. Once he got into the bumper car, the rest of the band and crew followed. They whirled for hours, and we couldn't get them out. We finally had to drag them from the place after two in the morning.

Phil's PR agent Sheryl Gordon with Jill Collins and daughter Lily Collins in 1990. I always looked forward to taking Jill and Sheryl out shopping for the afternoon when Phil was in town.

Jules with good friend Michael Farrell, agent with ITG. They represented Phil Collins, Genesis, Pink Floyd, Duran Duran, and Depeche Mode. Jules did many dates with Michael, and we were two of the 20 people at his wedding.

Mike + the Mechanics was a side project of Mike Rutherford, one of the founding members of Genesis.

When on hiatus from Genesis, Mike pursued a solo career to explore his own songwriting and to satisfy his urge to make music outside of the band. Mike + The Mechanics charted three Top 40 hits on their first album, including *All I Need is a Miracle*.

For this '89 shirt, we loved the idea of an authentic work shirt complete with embroidered patch—so did the band and crew.

April 17, 1989, Cleveland Palace Theatre

Billy Joel, October 29, 1986 ©Janet Macoska

These sweats were a hit with Billy and his crew.
Richfield Coliseum, March 1984

"Mr. Belkin," Bono called out, obviously not remembering Jules' first name.

It was right after the 2005 U2 show at Quicken Loans Arena, and Jules and I were walking to our car in the underground garage. Bono was getting into his SUV, too. He spotted Jules and called out, "Mr. Belkin!" The singer came right over with his hand out to shake Jules' hand. "We've been doing business together for 25 years and whenever I see your name on a contract, I know everything will be just right. Thank you!" Jules was so stunned, he just nodded and replied, "Uh, thank you." Bono jumped into his waiting car and was on his way.

> Everyone who worked backstage remembers the same story about the '85 show. The tour manager came out yelling about the towels; they were the wrong color and they were too small for a shower. Stacey told him we always got towels that were hand towel size...they weren't undernourished bath towels, Her solution to U2? Just use two towels for a shower.

Barry and Jules at a 2017 U2 Concert, First Energy Stadium

In the middle of the Unforgettable Fire tour, U2 moved from playing smaller halls to playing arenas. Their first Cleveland stop that tour was December 9, 1984 at the 3,000-seat Music Hall, and they returned March 25, 1985—just three months later— to entertain 17,000 concert-goers at the Richfield Coliseum.

U2

belkin productions

1984 - 85

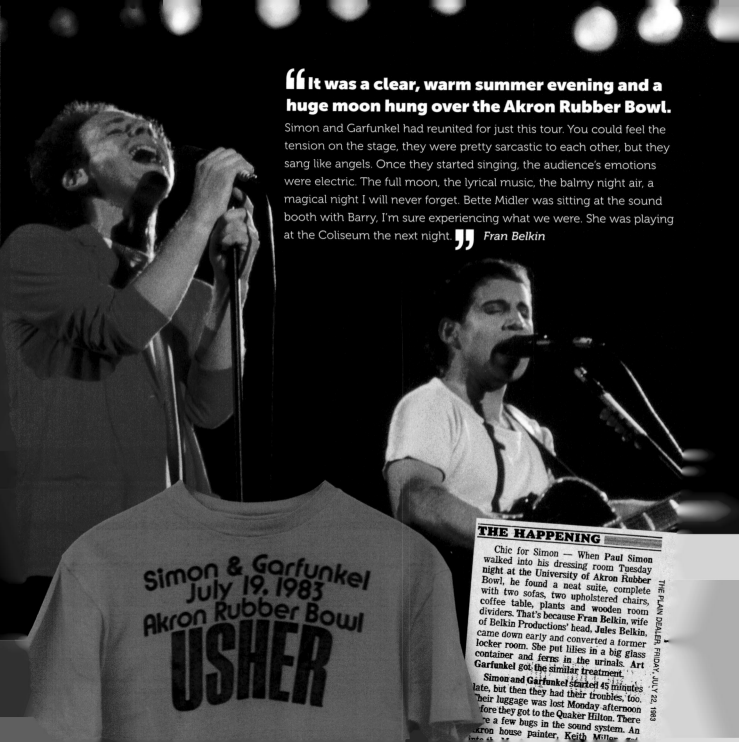

❝ It was a clear, warm summer evening and a huge moon hung over the Akron Rubber Bowl.

Simon and Garfunkel had reunited for just this tour. You could feel the tension on the stage, they were pretty sarcastic to each other, but they sang like angels. Once they started singing, the audience's emotions were electric. The full moon, the lyrical music, the balmy night air, a magical night I will never forget. Bette Midler was sitting at the sound booth with Barry, I'm sure experiencing what we were. She was playing at the Coliseum the next night. **❞** *Fran Belkin*

Simon & Garfunkel
July 19, 1983
Akron Rubber Bowl
USHER

THE HAPPENING

Chic for Simon — When **Paul Simon** walked into his dressing room Tuesday night at the University of Akron Rubber Bowl, he found a neat suite, complete with two sofas, two upholstered chairs, coffee table, plants and wooden room dividers. That's because **Fran Belkin**, wife of Belkin Productions' head, **Jules Belkin**, came down early and converted a former locker room. She put lilies in a big glass container and ferns in the urinals. **Art Garfunkel** got the similar treatment.

Simon and Garfunkel started 45 minutes late, but then they had their troubles, too. Their luggage was lost Monday afternoon before they got to the Quaker Hilton. There were a few bugs in the sound system. An Akron house painter, **Keith Miller**, got into th...

THE PLAIN DEALER, FRIDAY, JULY 22, 1983

When I was a young punk agent...
an email exchange with Jeff Kramer, longtime manager for Paul Simon

November 10-11, 2016

Hi Jeff: Fran and I can't thank you enough for the Paul Simon tix at Royal Albert Hall in London where we enjoyed one of the best concerts ever. We also were able to renew acquaintances with Mark Stewart and Jamey Haddad in the band. Brilliant set, an exuberant and appreciative audience made the evening one to remember.

Thanks again for remembering this old geezer and continuing good luck. Somewhere, someplace we'll see you again.*

Jules Belkin

Hi Jules: So happy I was able to take care of you and Fran. You'll always be "The Professor" to me. When I was a young punk agent you schooled me in lessons I've never forgotten. So, thank you for taking the time to educate me not just in deal-making, but in how to be a real professional in the business you helped build.

Love and best regards,
Jeff Kramer

"Somewhere, someplace" turned out to be backstage at Hollywood Bowl in 2018, where Jules took Fran on her birthday to see Paul Simon's Farewell Tour.

Left:
Simon & Garfunkel,
July 19, 1983
©Janet Macoska

Hello Jeff: I'm Jules' daughter and my mom passed your email along to me. I want to chime in to say your words to my dad are so thoughtful and special. It's not often that people take the time to write down kind words and pleasant memories. I know my dad will have a smile on his face and warmth in his heart from reading this.

Thank you!
Jamie Belkin

Hi Jamie: Thanks for the lovely note. Just so you know I meant every word of it. Your dad was not just one of the great pioneers of our business, he was an incredible person. Thoughtful, willing to teach, and always a pleasure to work with.

But the best thing about Jules was the influence he had on me and many others (Bobby Brooks, for example) in how he conducted himself. As tough as our business can be, he never lost his ability to be a wonderful human being. Don't get me wrong. He was tough and strong, but never a bully and never overbearing. It always felt like he was interested in what's fair and right, and not just winning for its own sake and in doing so he was a gift not only to our industry, but to humanity.

I will always be indebted and grateful to him for all that he imparted to me as a young man.

Best to you and your family,
Jeff Kramer

91

Bowling with Van Halen

Sammy Hagar had just joined the band, and their new album *5150* was moving up the charts. (Incidentally, 5150 is the California law enforcement code for a mentally disturbed person, hence the straitjackets).

The Van Halen band and crew eagerly put on their bowling shirts and came over to the party right after the show. And of course, the entire Belkin office came, too.

Steve and Jamie Belkin

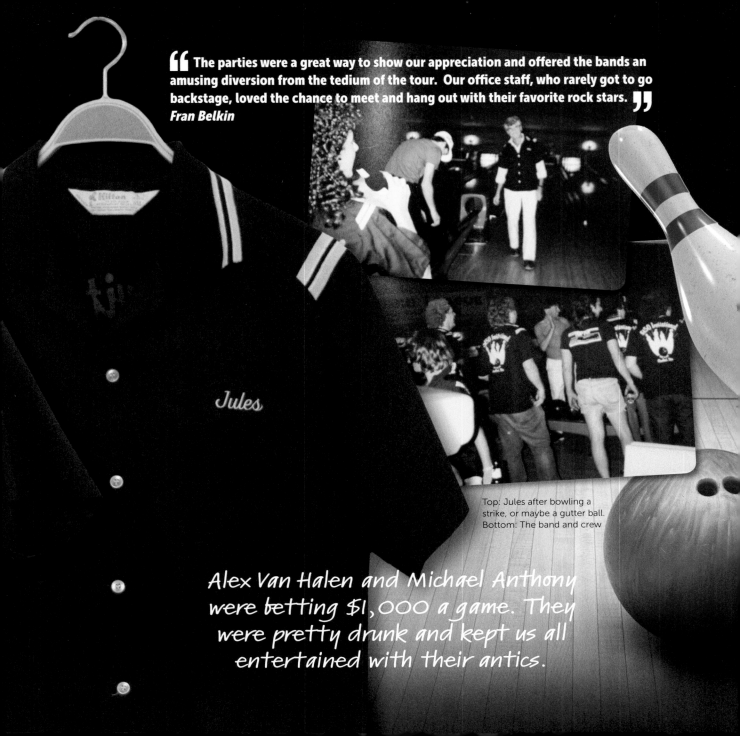

> **The parties were a great way to show our appreciation and offered the bands an amusing diversion from the tedium of the tour. Our office staff, who rarely got to go backstage, loved the chance to meet and hang out with their favorite rock stars.**
> *Fran Belkin*

Top: Jules after bowling a strike, or maybe a gutter ball.
Bottom: The band and crew

Alex Van Halen and Michael Anthony were betting $1,000 a game. They were pretty drunk and kept us all entertained with their antics.

So John, what projects are you working on?

Jules wasn't one to drop into the band's dressing room unless he had a relationship with the band members. He was there to do his job, oversee the production and do the settlement with the accountant. But The Who were old friends, so he went in to say hello. He dragged me with him and I stood there feeling stupid, but then I remembered an article I had just read about how to start a conversation with someone who intimidates you: you ask what projects they are working on. John Entwhistle was standing closest to me, so I turned to him and asked him if he was working on anything special now. He gave me a big smile and said he was doing something called a Soup Diet, eating nothing but soup, and he had lost 10 pounds! He seemed quite pleased to be asked something unrelated to The Who. I have used that question many times since.

The Who, July 19, 1989,
Cleveland Stadium

Jules had heard a story about Pete and Roger being seen in the hallway of the hotel Plaza Athénée in Paris in their undershorts. Jules said, "They need bathrobes!" He proceeded to find the heaviest, most luxurious robes he could, and had them embroidered. They were just for the band members. The crew got a thick sweatshirt with their anniversary logo (and of course, the Belkin logo on the back).

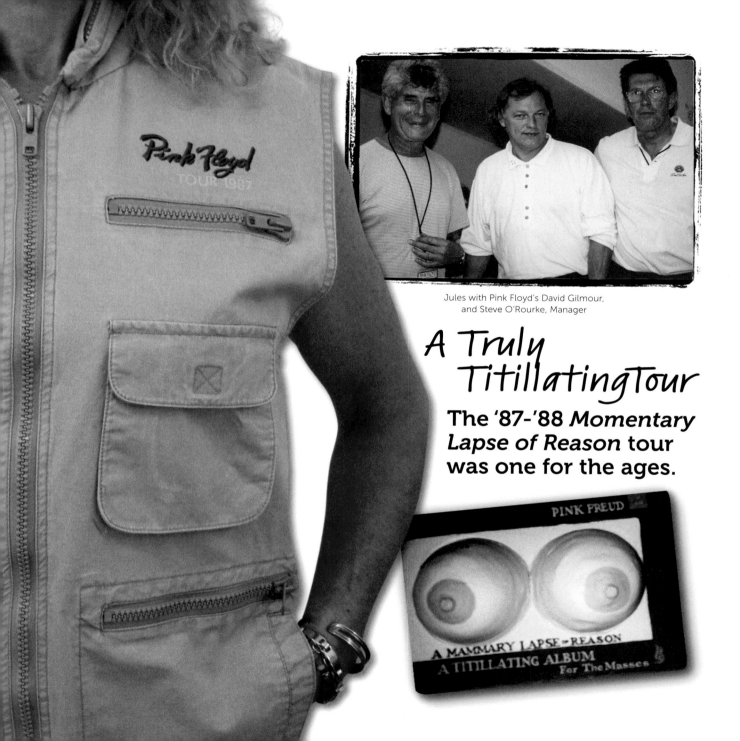

Jules with Pink Floyd's David Gilmour,
and Steve O'Rourke, Manager

A Truly Titillating Tour

The '87-'88 *Momentary Lapse of Reason* tour was one for the ages.

PINK FREUD

A MAMMARY LAPSE = REASON
A TITILLATING ALBUM For The Masses

After vowing for years to never host rock concerts in their esteemed stadium, Ohio State invited Belkin Productions to do their first ever rock show. This was a huge compliment to Belkin Productions and Jules knew the band he wanted....Pink Floyd had the popularity and the prestige for this momentous occasion. And they were available for that date with their Momentary Lapse of Reason tour.

Jules, a Michigan alum, was gleeful as the crews built the stage on the field over what was reputed to be the grave of Woody Hayes (famed Ohio State football coach). Sunny skies and a stadium full of jubilant fans welcomed Pink Floyd the day of the concert. It was an enthusiastic audience for an exceptional performance, and the band was ecstatic as they came off the stage. Their manager, Steve O'Rourke, asked Barry, "What can I do to thank Jules?" And, as only Barry can, he responded, "Just give him more shows!"

So when Pink Floyd came back to the States after touring the world, they played only two cities: Cleveland and Detroit—both for Belkin—before ending the tour by recording their live album. We had a rollicking party with a very sassy cake. What a jovial bash that was, with the band and crew celebrating that they would be soon heading home to England. David Gilmour told Jules he was happy to be ending the tour with good friends.

The Faces of Rock and Roll

They say a picture's worth a thousand words, and for a few years in the early '80s we added pictures and caricatures to some of the t-shirts. Distinctive faces like those of Roy Orbison, Frank Zappa, and the guys in Cheap Trick were naturals for caricatures and added a sense of humor to the swag.

Cheap Trick, 1978, Richfield Coliseum ©Janet Macoska
Polaroid: Belkin's Wendy Stein having a laugh with the band.

GEORGE MICHAEL
FAITH TOUR
1988

belkin
productions

CLEVELAND
DETROIT
LEXINGTON

"Crews always looked forward to Belkin swag— it was well-designed, good quality and fun." *Roy Clair*

Stacey and I would brainstorm ideas and come up with designs for the swag. The artwork for George Michael, Tina Turner and Rod Stewart were so original that these shirts became rock stars themselves thanks to our designer, Leo Schleicher.

Rod Stewart's 1988 Out of Order tour opened with bagpipe players marching down the aisles, and then Rod came out kicking a soccer ball around the stage. He finally kicked it out into the audience and the music started.

> ❝ Rick Springfield had a radio promotion where people were supposed to meet the rock star and get his autograph. But immediately after the show, Rick took off and I was stuck with the excited fans.
>
> I pushed Tom (Einhouse) into the dressing room with the stack of Rick's headshots and told him to 'sign them like a rock star!' He signed them all and added a flourish, dotting the 'i' in Springfield with a star. Then, feeling a little guilt but not wanting to totally disappoint Rick's fans, I handed them out. ❞ *Stacey Harper*

> ❝ Ray Davies from the Kinks had come to the hall early. I was preparing cheese trays for the dressing rooms and Ray just sat down with me and talked about how much he loved Cleveland. He said the music scene in Cleveland is so vibrant, and WMMS and Belkin does a great job promoting his band. I couldn't believe Ray Davies was sitting down across from me and chatting like we were friends! ❞ *Tom Einhouse*

Following his college-era job as a Belkin runner, Tom was hired by Playhouse Square in 1980. He is now Vice President of Real Estate Development for the nation's second largest performing arts complex.

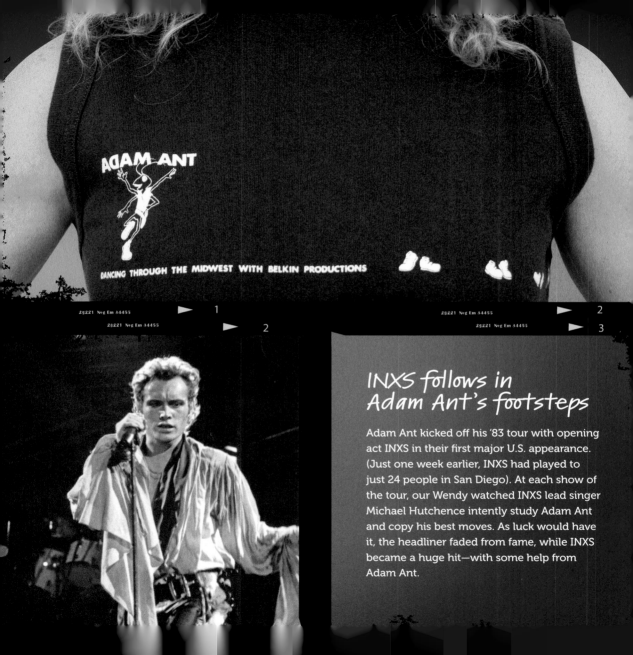

ADAM ANT

DANCING THROUGH THE MIDWEST WITH BELKIN PRODUCTIONS

INXS follows in Adam Ant's footsteps

Adam Ant kicked off his '83 tour with opening act INXS in their first major U.S. appearance. (Just one week earlier, INXS had played to just 24 people in San Diego). At each show of the tour, our Wendy watched INXS lead singer Michael Hutchence intently study Adam Ant and copy his best moves. As luck would have it, the headliner faded from fame, while INXS became a huge hit—with some help from Adam Ant.

So many ways to say Yes!

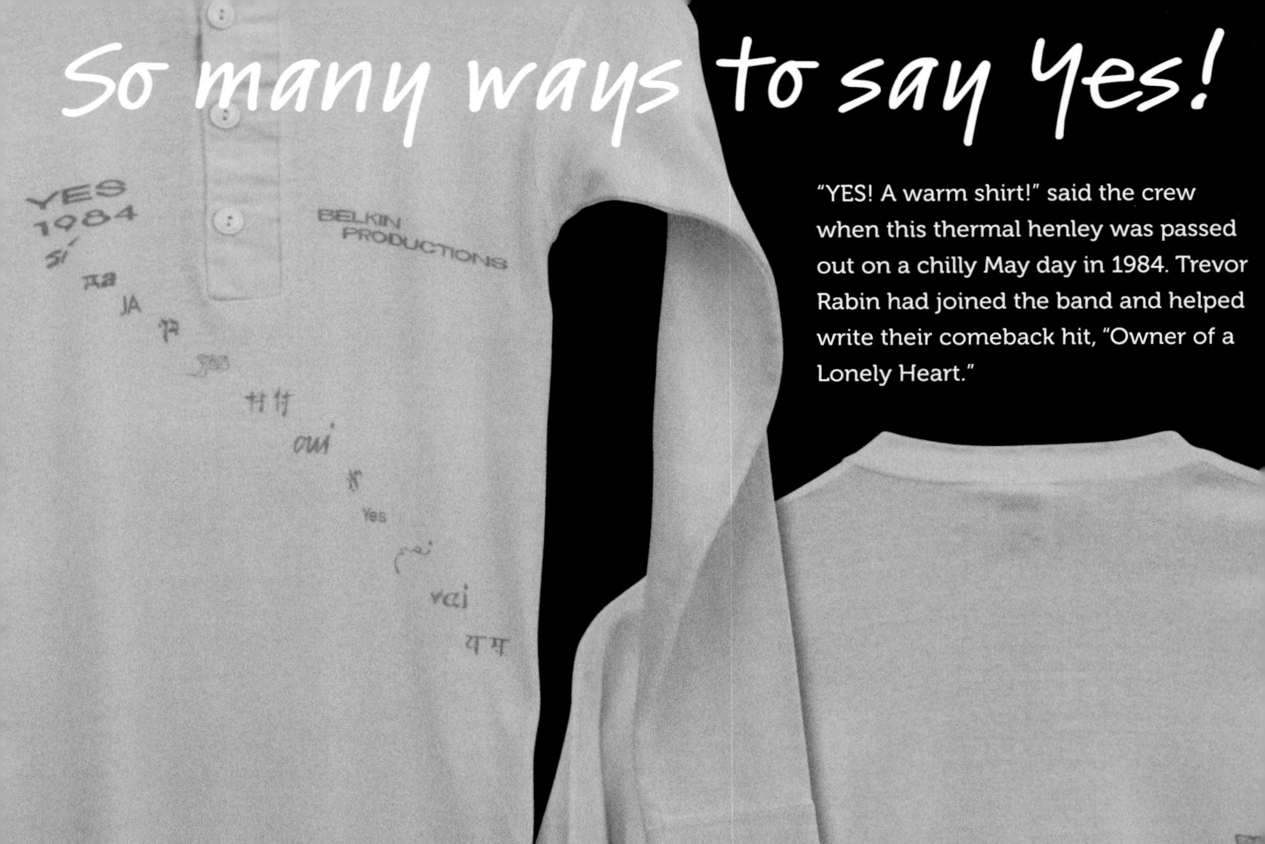

YES
1984
sí
па
JA
오
유
所以
म
oui
유
Yes
उ
vai
य प

BELKIN
PRODUCTIONS

"YES! A warm shirt!" said the crew when this thermal henley was passed out on a chilly May day in 1984. Trevor Rabin had joined the band and helped write their comeback hit, "Owner of a Lonely Heart."

Irene Reveno, Fran's mother

य प
NDIYO
Jaa
에
ग्ट
TAK

" My mother Irene had met Trevor Rabin in South Africa and called Jules to sing his praises: 'Trevor is such a talented musician. You should try to manage him.' Jules rolled his eyes as if to say, *'What do you know about rock music?'* The next thing we knew, Rabin had joined YES and spurred the band's resurgence. **"** *Fran Belkin*

> Bon Jovi was the top band in the land in '87 when Jon told his manager Doc McGhee that he wanted to do a show in Erie, where his mother grew up and his grandmother still lived. Doc asked me to book it. The biggest venue in Erie was the high school football stadium. It was big news in Erie, and an incredible concert. People came from all over the region, and no one sat down the entire concert! *Jules Belkin*

Tico Torres and Jon Bon Jovi at WMMS, c. 1984 ©Janet Macoska

Oh, can you pay us in cash?

It was July 4th, 1989 weekend, and the bands had all asked for payment in cash for the shows at Buckeye Lake and Akron Rubber Bowl. So on Friday before the weekend, Betsy Delis, Jules' assistant, and Denny Young, marketing guy, went to the bank to get $300,000, stuffed into large canvas bags. Denny put the bulging sacks in the trunk of his car and fretted all night about his car sitting in his apartment's garage. When he picked Jules up Saturday morning for the drive to Buckeye Lake, he was relieved to report that the money was still there!

Jules with Cher at the Rubber Bowl. At the time, she was dating Richie Sambora of Bon Jovi. (Coincidentally, Cher had dated the lead singer of opening act Winger a few years earlier.) She and Jules were happy to cross paths again.

105

I
WORSHIPED
AT THE
HEAVY METAL
ALTAR

BELKIN PRODUCTIONS PRESENTS
"POINT OF ENTRY" TOUR 1981

APRIL 30, 1981 — ERIE COUNTY FIELDHOUSE
MAY 1, 1981 — RICHFIELD COLISEUM

Heavy Metal
Madness

Rob Halford of Judas Priest, 1982 ©Janet Macoska

Belkin PRODUCTIONS, FM 104 STEREO & Budweiser KING OF BEERS

WELCOME

IRON MAIDEN

FASTWAY

— special guest —

CONEY HATCH
HEAVY METAL FEAST
TOLEDO SPORTS ARENA
SAT., SEPT. 10 7:30 P.M.

We made these short shorts for Mötley Crüe in response to the line in the song Girls, Girls, Girls: "long legs and burgundy lips."

Crüesin'

belkin productions

" After the show started, Stacey and I would sometimes go out to the concourse, grab a hot dog, and walk around. One night, we turned the corner to see the deputy sheriffs chasing down a kid. When they caught him, the pills and drugs went flying. They handcuffed and gathered him into the elevator. 'Let's take the elevator, too,' Stacey said. We got on and the doors closed behind us. Stacey looked at the kid, smiled, and said, 'So, you enjoy the show?' " *Tom Einhouse*

> **Jules has always had a very unique talent, an eye and an ear for things no other promoter would touch—until he showed them that it would work. He was first with many acts, including the Moscow Circus, which he successfully booked all over the country. But his biggest success was the Trans- Siberian Orchestra—still one of the biggest acts touring the world. He was the first one to take a chance on them.** *Phil Ober*

Shows that did more than rock.

**Moscow Circus • La Cage aux Folles • Lord of the Dance • Lippizan Stallions
Jesus Christ Superstar • Oh! Calcutta! • Motorcycles on Ice • The Male Intellect**

Billy Joel and the Cossack Stunt Rider

In 1987, Billy became the first American performer to tour the Soviet Union after they opened their doors. On an off night during the tour, Billy took wife Christie and daughter Alexa to see the Moscow Circus. After the show, the troupe invited Billy and family backstage, and the Nugzarov Troupe of Cossack stunt riders let Alexa ride one of the horses around the ring. Meanwhile Billy got to know one of the stunt riders, Beres. A few years later, Barry got wind of the story during the Moscow Circus run in Chicago. He flew Beres to Cleveland to reunite with his friend. Billy was thrilled to see him.

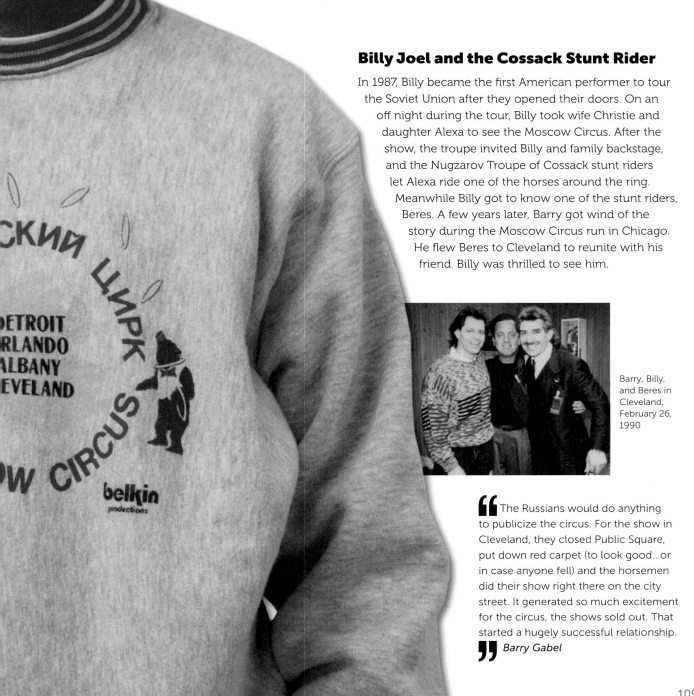

Barry, Billy, and Beres in Cleveland, February 26, 1990

❝ The Russians would do anything to publicize the circus. For the show in Cleveland, they closed Public Square, put down red carpet (to look good...or in case anyone fell) and the horsemen did their show right there on the city street. It generated so much excitement for the circus, the shows sold out. That started a hugely successful relationship. **❞** *Barry Gabel*

The Pentecostal Preacher Turned Comedian

Elliot Abbott, Kinks agent and Jules' long time friend, called to say his client Sam Kinison was playing the Cleveland Comedy Club and asked us to catch his show. Sam was hilarious, with great timing and a smart riff delivered with the charismatic intensity he'd honed as a preacher—punctuated by his trademark scream. Jules and Barry were sold, and immediately took a bunch of dates. Jules was the only promoter booking Sam—all over the eastern half of the country. The jacket was pricey swag, but it was the least we could do for a guy who was selling out everywhere and was loyal to Belkin.

Sam Kinison (wearing our varsity jacket) flashes the time out sign with Barry.

"I told Sam Kinison that he couldn't keep showing up so late to the show. We risked getting big union penalties if the show started too late. His response? He started doing the time out sign and saying 'Wait, Barry, The show doesn't start until I say it does. I need another time out!'**"** *Barry Gabel*

Jules takes a chance on TSO

"They're a new band called Trans-Siberian Orchestra," David Krebs had said. "You need to get up here to see them." Jules was intrigued. His close friendship with David Krebs extended back through his managing Aerosmith, the Scorpions and Ted Nugent. Jules headed to New York to see this "concept concert," which told the Christmas story accompanied by traditional Christmas songs—but translated into rock music. The entire production was so compelling and uplifting that Jules immediately said he would book it and took the first five shows.

In Cleveland, Barry gave WNCX the promotion because they had been playing TSO's music and were getting lots of positive feedback. Jules told Barry to start calling other markets to partner with us: Detroit, Chicago, Philly and others. The promoters were leery but agreed to the bookings if they were guaranteed not to lose money. Jules said he would cover any downside and would share in the profit. They all said "You bet!"

The first show in Cleveland sold out immediately, but Music Hall wasn't available the next night so they booked the second night at Playhouse Square. That sold out quickly, too. The next night wasn't available *there* so they went back to Music Hall for the third date. Three load-ins and three load-outs in three days!

By 2017, TSO was selling one million tickets a year and had been nicknamed the "Rock and Roll Nutcracker." It was Jules' biggest success...and all from a group that originally sold its album on the QVC shopping network.

TSO's director of touring and production Elliot Saltzman, Fran, agent Marc Geiger, Jules, manager Adam Lind, Barry Gabel, and Adam's wife Alicia at TSO 2018

Times were different in 1984 when the Tony-award winning musical *La Cage aux Folles* toured. It was a hit in New York. Jules loved the show but feared it might be too avant garde for Cleveland. He decided to chance it. The promotion had to engender a lot of publicity, so he and Mike dressed in drag for the press conference on the stage at Music Hall. They got huge press, but the show still didn't sell. However, the photos were so much fun we decided to use one for our company Christmas card, with the message...

Don we now our gay apparel ...fa-la-la-la-la, la-la-la-la.

GREG JIRA

Rider, what Ryder? I didn't rent a truck for this show.

FRAN BELKIN

Another card another card

JIM LASHER

Belkin Accounting

2 + 2 = 3

DAN KEMER

I'd like to wish you a happy holiday, but let me check with Barry first

BARRY GABEL

I never inhaled either!

Happy, Happy Joy, Joy

STACEY HARPER

I'm checking the backstage guest list twice, to find out who's been naughty or nice!

JAMIE BELKIN

Hope your festivals are full of "baby" back ribs, "little" tike hoops, and a "little" bit of country.

BETSY DELIS

You better not shout, You better not cry, You better not pout... or you're not getting your deposit!

JULES BELKIN

I don't rememb[...] saying that!

A favorite Belkin Productions holiday card, artwork by Leo Schleicher, 1992.

Raising the curtain in Chagrin Falls

After paying rent for decades and a gradual migration east of downtown Cleveland, we bought an old building in the charming suburb of Chagrin Falls. For the first time, we were the landlord. After an extensive renovation, the company settled happily into our new home. To celebrate, we welcomed our family, friends, and associates with a party that December.

belkin productions

Mike and Jules
Are raising the curtain on
the new office in Chagrin Falls
Please join us for an
Open House
Monday, December 21, 1987
5 - 9 p.m.

R.S.V.P.
to Sheri
247-2722

MIKE BELKIN
Happy Christmas
Merry Hanukkah
Still confused after all these years.

AMY DAWSON
Hope your stocking is stuffed with Donnie Iris and Michael Stanley CD's.

PAM BARKER
Wishing all of our sponsors a "sell-out" holiday and one more banner in a high traffic area.

PATTI del VILLAN
Wishing you two of my favorite things: good seats, no complaints.

JOHN ROGERS
Wishing you maximum exposure in 1993.

MICHAEL BELKIN
92's done and still sold dodged my 32nd bullet

ANNE O'DONNELL
Wishing you a very happy. . . Could you please hold?

PHIL OBER
After 20 years I finally made it on the Christmas Card

Happy Holidays

Picnics & Belkin Tees for our Championship Team

Every summer Mike and Jules hosted a picnic for the office staff and the bands Mike managed. These summer picnics at Mike's were one of the reasons we all loved to work at Belkin Productions. The huge property with a lake, a tennis court and lots of grassy areas was the perfect spot to kick back and have fun together away from backstage or the office. Michael Stanley always organized a baseball game (we all wanted to be on his team) and there was lots of food, cold beer and good cheer.

One year, Mike told us he had a surprise for us, but we had to wait until dark. After sunset, a 10-foot square bed of charcoal was doused in lighter fluid and lit with a match. It erupted in flames. The guy who lit the fire explained that he was a team building coach, and we were all about to walk across hot coals. While the flames roared, he did his best to convince us that if we made up our minds not to get burned, we wouldn't.

Once the flames subsided and the coals were glowing red, he suggested Mike walk across first.

"Be confident," the guru said with authority. Mike walked the hot coals. One by one, most of us followed *(quickly)*. We survived unscathed and we all became believers of mind over matter!

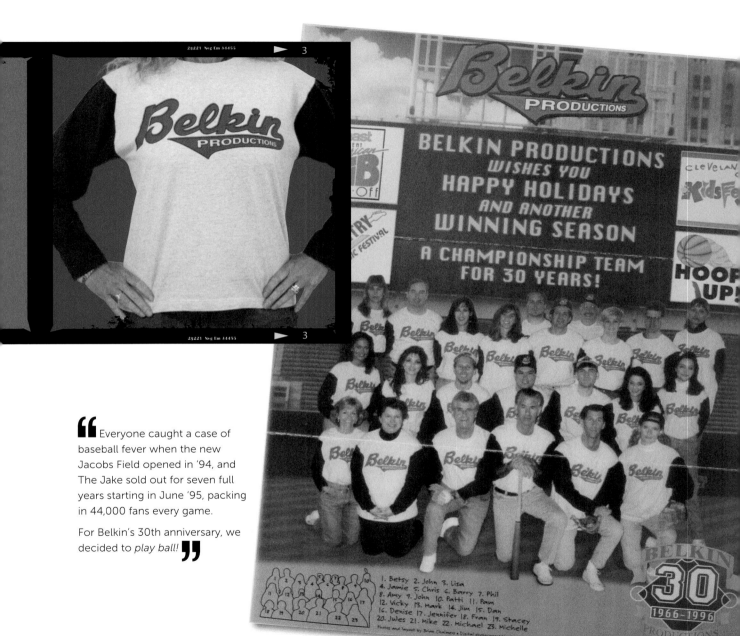

> Everyone caught a case of baseball fever when the new Jacobs Field opened in '94, and The Jake sold out for seven full years starting in June '95, packing in 44,000 fans every game.
>
> For Belkin's 30th anniversary, we decided to *play ball!*

BELKIN PRODUCTIONS WISHES YOU HAPPY HOLIDAYS AND ANOTHER WINNING SEASON

A CHAMPIONSHIP TEAM FOR 30 YEARS!

1. Betsy 2. John 3. Lisa
4. Jamie 5. Chris 6. Barry 7. Phil
8. Amy 9. John 10. Patti 11. Pam
12. Vicky 13. Mark 14. Jim 15. Dan
16. Denise 17. Jennifer 18. Fran 19. Stacey
20. Jules 21. Mike 22. Michael 23. Michelle

Photos and layout by Brian Chalmers • Digital photocomposition by Joe Holman & Dave Fetcher @ Holman Digital Design

BELKIN 30 1966-1996 PRODUCTIONS

Nautica Stage

Opened in 1987, Nautica was a spectacular open air venue right on the curve of Cleveland's Cuyahoga River next to the Powerhouse. For 13 seasons, Belkin was the exclusive booker.

The much-anticipated opening show at Nautica was starring South Side Johnny and the Asbury Jukes—but just before show time it started raining, hard. Although the stage was covered, the fans weren't and everyone ran for cover. But no one left, and when the rain slowed to a drizzle, a grateful South Side Johnny came out and played 12 songs, all with RAIN in the title: *Purple Rain, Singing in the Rain, Fire and Rain*, even *It's Raining Men*. The audience happily sang along. Eventually the rain stopped completely and they did their regular set.

Pat McKinley's Top 3 Nautica Memories

Pat is EVP of Jacobs Entertainment, and has run Nautica since it opened

3 Lou Reed arrived early for the sound check before his '89 show. He looked a little wobbly onstage, and as he came off the stage he missed a step and fell down the stairs. An ambulance took him to the hospital...bad news, he had a broken ankle. Jules was forced to cancel the show; it was close to a sell-out and people were already lined up to get in. Refunds were given and we instructed our parking people to refund the $4 for parking as the disappointed fans left.

Weeks later Jules got the news that Lou Reed was suing him for *lack of consortium* because he said the accident had affected him in a mental way and impaired his sexual ability. Needless to say, he never played for Belkin again.

2 Courtney Love opened for Nine Inch Nails in '94. During her set, she took her top off and marched around the stage bare-breasted, and the audience went crazy. The police must have been tipped off, because they were waiting to arrest her. I held them off with a promise she wouldn't do that at the next night's show. I made sure she didn't.

1 Stone Temple Pilots played in '94. The security guards stood outside the mosh pit, ready to pull people out if they got in trouble. This night, they brought out a guy who was curled up on the floor, drunk and incoherent. He wouldn't stand up and kept asking for something. The security guard finally realized he was asking for his wheelchair!

The unfortunate fan had been at the side of the mosh pit when he was picked up and passed around overhead—before being dropped. The guards located his wheelchair and put him in it, but he was so drunk he just kept rolling in circles. They finally got him into a taxi to take him home.

Outdoor Festivals

After Jules' daughter Jamie graduated college in 1987, she started working for Cleveland event management and production company Salls & Bonda, who planned an outdoor festival called Riverfest. It was a multi-day event along the Cuyahoga River. After two years, the owners dissolved the partnership and Jamie brought her extensive outdoor experience to Belkin Productions. The management of the National Rib Cook Off was soon up for grabs, and between Jamie's festival production background and Barry's knowledge and creativity for packaging sponsorships, Jules and Mike decided to give it a go. Along with the newly named Great American Rib Cook Off, the Belkin summer event season grew to include KidsFest, Country Music Festival, and eventually A Taste of Cleveland.

The Flats RiverFest Corporation: The Team Behind The Scene. Dewey Forward, Entertainment; Dick Clough, Marketing; Ron Waldhager, Legal; Jamie Belkin, Special Projects; Tom Bonda, President.

> " Admission to A Taste of Cleveland was a great deal: $6 with entertainment included. Between the date we booked Barenaked Ladies and the night of the 1987 festival, the Canadian band's popularity took off. The event reached capacity, and we were forced to stop selling tickets. That didn't stop some BNL fans. They made a dash for the fence and climbed over faster than our security could stop them. Total chaos ensued! " *Jamie Belkin*

Barenaked Ladies on stage, August 30, 1987

For more than a decade, Belkin summers were packed with outdoor concerts and a strong festival line-ups. Michael booked the bands ranging from the Goo Goo Dolls and Barenaked Ladies, to Eddie Money, Shania Twain and Marky Mark. Stacey did all the concert production. A few of the acts were booked months prior to the events and had huge hits in the interim, which meant strong ticket and beer sales.

Mike looked at the events as more than just food, beverage and concert ticket sales. He saw the opportunity for people to spend more money while at the events, so he invested in carnival games and various branded merchandise. His daughter Lisa managed the games and the merchandise store. Along with other responsibilities, she scheduled the staff, which included Mike's wife Annie and their son Sam. At any given time, Belkin offspring would be collecting money at the high-striker, duck pond, fast pitch or beer slide.

The entire Belkin team stepped in to pour beer when needed.

Sam and Annie

Great American Rib Cook-Off

The fledgling Rib Cook-Off needed press, so the brothers were photographed with sauce mustaches, and Barry had a special label designed for the BBQ sauce, which they sent to local media. The Rib Cook-off got the big coverage they hoped for...every TV station in town did a story.

finast scenes from the **GREAT AMERICAN RIB COOK-OFF**

pig pen

pigmy

piggy banker

pig's feet

elvis pigley

pig out

piggy back

pigskin

benedict arnold ziffel

burke lakefront airport · may 25-29, 1995
cleveland, ohio

The brothers were at it again!

Faith Hill, 1995
©Janet Macoska

Country Music Festival

"It's been decades since Tim McGraw, Faith Hill and Toby Keith all performed on the same line-up, but at Country Fest '95 they shared the stage. Today they each can sell out a stadium. And Tim and Faith married just months later." *Jules Belkin*

PEPSI
COUNTRY
MUSIC FESTIVAL

THE TRACTORS
BLACKHAWK
KATHY MATTEA
HAL KETCHUM
TIM McGRAW
TOBY KEITH
JOHN BERRY
FAITH HILL
RUSS TAFF
BRYAN WHITE
JUNE 16·17·18·1995

> **Producing events isn't all glitz and glamour. I learned by example from my dad, Jules. In the early days, he helped set up and number the chairs on the field at the stadium concerts. He taught me to do whatever was necessary to get the job done...even picking up trash.**
> *Jamie Belkin*

Jamie folding chairs following a late 1980s outdoor festival.

The small but mighty Belkin Productions special events team in 2000. Barry, Jen Climer, Jamie, Jim Lasher, Trevor Ralph, and Jamie's daughter Dylan.

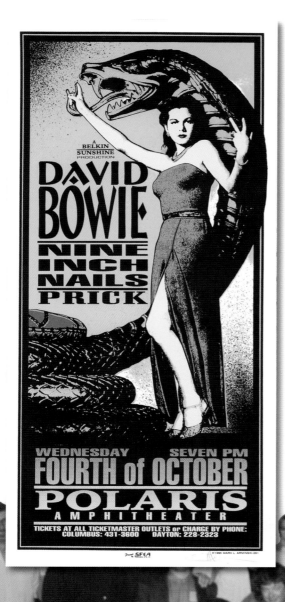

A BELKIN SUNSHINE PRODUCTION

DAVID BOWIE
NINE INCH NAILS
PRICK

WEDNESDAY   SEVEN PM
FOURTH of OCTOBER
POLARIS
AMPHITHEATER

TICKETS AT ALL TICKETMASTER OUTLETS or CHARGE BY PHONE:
COLUMBUS: 431-3600   DAYTON: 228-2323

Owning a concert venue was Jules' dream. In 1994, it became his reality: Polaris Amphitheater.

By the late '80s, concert promoters from throughout the US and Canada began meeting. It was nothing short of a miracle for these competitors (enemies?) to be in one room, asking themselves, what can we do together to make our businesses better? Many were in overlapping territories and were bidding up the price of acts just to get the show. Maybe they could work together? They were also buying individual insurance for shows, and if they banded together they could buy as a group and save. This was an exciting first step.

Dave Lucas of Sunshine Productions (from Indianapolis) and Jules had a chance to talk and they both thought Columbus needed a big outdoor amphitheater. They each booked Columbus as competitors, so they decided to build a venue together. Belkin Productions had always booked venues owned by others, and here was the opportunity to finally own one. It would be called Polaris.

Jules went to Columbus every week during the build-out of Polaris and was very active in the facility design, from giant loading docks to accommodate the huge semis the bands used now to women's bathrooms twice the size of the men's rooms so the girls weren't waiting in line as they were in every other facility (hooray!). Even the landscaping was exceptional. The parking lots were grass instead of blacktop so it felt like a park. The fan experience was paramount in his plan for Polaris.

When Polaris opened in June 1994, it was a dream come true for Jules. Everything about Polaris was first class and, led by general manager Patrick Leahy, the amphitheater was a huge success. Polaris became the must-play venue in the Midwest for bands. The Eagles played their reunion gig at Polaris, David Bowie, Steely Dan, the Allman Brothers, all the best bands stopped in Columbus.

Hell froze over twice.

After Joe Walsh left the James Gang in 1971, hard feelings developed between Joe and Mike Belkin. Joe said he wouldn't play for Belkin again *'until hell freezes over.'* Walsh joined The Eagles, and when that band later split up in 1980, Don Henley insisted they wouldn't get back together *'until hell freezes over.'* In August 1994, hell froze over not once, but twice. The Eagles had reunited and were playing Polaris—for Belkin Productions!

❝ That night, when Joe Walsh sang *Rocky Mountain Way*, he changed the words from:

Bases are loaded, Casey's at bat, Time to change the pitcher

— to —

Bases are loaded, Belkin's at bat, Time to change the promoter! ❞

Steve Belkin

Left: Concert promoters' meeting, Miami 1988. Jules, third from right. Dave Lucas, fourth from right. Above left: A rare screenprinted poster designed by Mark Arminski for Polaris, October 4, 1995 ©Mark Arminski, arminski.com

"You could fit a corpse in it!"

(This was the largest piece of swag we ever produced—and the most coveted. Crew members told us they'd never check it at the airport because they knew they'd never see it again.)

> In '94, I was a student at the University of Wisconsin in Madison, and I got a part time job with RTM Security (that's short for Real Tough Men). Belkin Productions would hire us to handle security and logistics for the big rock shows at the university's stadium, Camp Randall.
>
> At the Pink Floyd show, I made a decision to have the band's semis moved from an off-site parking lot to the VIP lot on-site to save time for the load out (I knew time was money when you're talking stagehands). Jamie Belkin, production coordinator for the show, came by and saw what I'd done: The spots were needed for the VIPs to park and she was going to be in big trouble. I had to think on my feet and fix the problem—and quick.
>
> So I got a bunch of my college buddies to act as valet attendants. We parked the cars around and even under the semis. In the end, it all worked out and guests were impressed and surprised to receive "valet" service. *Brian Zimmerman, CEO Metroparks Cleveland*

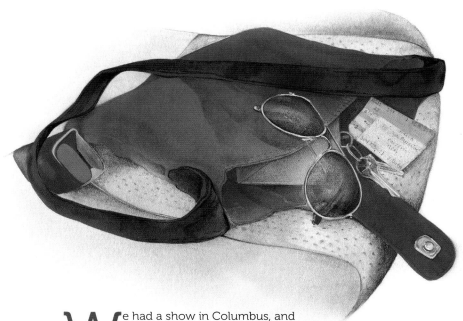

We had a show in Columbus, and it was a nasty night with freezing rain and sleet. The cars were slipping and sliding trying to get into the parking lot, and some people didn't make it inside the venue until intermission.

Jules told the box office staff to refund anyone's ticket who didn't get in to see the entire show.

"Make it right," he said.

The next morning, Jules called down to Columbus and asked the box office manager how things had gone, and how many tickets he had refunded. The manager reported that there were only a few refunds, but one woman wants you to buy her a new purse.

Jules said "Huh?"

"You're not going to believe this one," said the box office manager. "She said she waited so long to get into the parking lot, and she had to go to the bathroom so badly, she ended up peeing in her purse. And she wants you to buy her a new one."

Barenaked Ladies and the Misplaced Passport

Barenaked Ladies had played Chicago and were heading to Cleveland the next day on their tour bus. Since there was an extra day off before the Cleveland show, lead singer Eddie Robertson decided to fly home to Toronto to see his family.

When he arrived in Toronto, he panicked...he had left his passport on the bus and couldn't get back into the U.S. without it. When the bus arrived in Cleveland, Bob Ferrell, our runner (then and now), grabbed the passport and drove to the Canadian border near Buffalo. A grateful Eddie Robertson was waiting on the other side.

> BNL had the #1 song on the US charts that week with *One Week*. It remained atop the charts for, yep, one week. 🙶

Personalized satin jackets given to us by Budweiser distributors and long time partners House of LaRose, c. 1994

WMMS BELKIN *Budweiser* CONCERTS

" Shameless hucksters that we were, we gave a few to WMMS for on-air promotion, too. " *Jim LaRose*

Fran, Jim LaRose, president of House of LaRose beverage distributor, Jules, and Don George, lead salesman for Budweiser, at the 80th birthday party for Jane Scott at Odeon Night Club.

Shameless hucksters that WE ARE, we're including this jacket we didn't design. Budweiser sales paid a lot of bills! *Fran Belkin*

Michele and Michael get Satisfaction

In the summer of 1994, we were promoting a number of Rolling Stones dates including a show in Indianapolis. My nephew Michael's girlfriend Michele was a huge fan so he thought it would be the perfect place to propose.

Michael asked for help from the tour manager, who said, "Come to the Voodoo Lounge to propose and I'll arrange everything". Michael was stunned when the tour manager grabbed the diamond engagement ring and left. When Michael told Michele that they were invited up to the band's lounge, she was ecstatic.

Once in the lounge, they were chatting with the tour manager when Keith Richards casually walked up and asked, "So, are you two married?"

Surprised, Michele said, "No."

Keith grinned and pulled the diamond ring from his pocket and said, "Well, you oughta be!"

Now it was Michele's turn to be shocked. Between laughter and tears, Michele found herself surrounded by the entire band and the man should she would later marry. It was definitely a special proposal.

Friends in the Business

We went to the 1988 promoters' meeting in Miami with Rich Engler, the promoter from Pittsburgh, and his wife Cindy, whom I had never met. Cindy and I became fast friends. As backstage wives we shared a common bond: spending much of our lives hanging out at concerts, meeting rock stars, and protecting our men from young girls who would do anything to get backstage.

In the photo above, Rich and Cindy joined us at the Rock & Roll Hall of Fame while they were in Cleveland for the 2015 Induction Ceremonies.

Terry Stewart (then Rock Hall director), Fran, Jules, Cindy and Rich Engler, and Joel Peresman, CEO of the Rock & Roll Hall of Fame Foundation

Concert for the Rock & Roll Hall of Fame, 1995

Belkin is behind 'once-in-a-lifetime' event

By JEFF PIORKOWSKI
Staff Writer

Performers have their quirks. Just ask **Jules Belkin**, who remembers all the fuss when Frank Sinatra came to town in 1969.

"Basically, Sinatra wanted us to re-create Caesars Palace in his dressing room at Public Hall," recalls Belkin, who, with brother Mike, heads Belkin Productions, Cleveland's top concert promotions agency. "We had to put in an air conditioner — it was a very primitive dressing area — and we had to knock a hole in the wall to do it because there was no window in the room. We redecorated and had Italian restaurants all over Cleveland calling to ask what they could bring.

"Then, when it was all done and we had gone through all this trouble, he ended up staying in that room about 10 minutes before he went on stage. That was it."

Still, Belkin, 64, recalls his 30 years in the business with relish. He also relishes the concert which will be seen around the world at 7:30 p.m. Sept. 2 from Cleveland Stadium. Televised by HBO, it will feature more than 30 acts, all on hand to celebrate the opening of the Rock and Roll Hall of Fame.

Artists such as Aretha Franklin, Bruce Springsteen, the Pretenders, Jerry Lee Lewis, Little Richard and the Allman Brothers will perform

ROCK 'N' ROLL COUNTDOWN 22

duets in still unknown combinations, lending an air of surprise to the one-of-a-kind show.

At a July 31 media reception at the Hall of Fame, Belkin said, "Artists all over the world are calling each other right now, asking what they're going to perform together.

"Can you imagine the power of Bruce Springsteen teaming up with the 'Godfather of Soul,' James Brown? It could happen at this concert. Or, Aretha Franklin burning up the stage with Melissa Etheridge? It could happen here."

Belkin, who lists Phil Collins and former Led Zeppelin lead singer Robert Plant as two of the nicer people with whom he has worked, enjoys the excitement his job can bring to others.

"We did the Rolling Stones at the Stadium in 1978," he said. "There were 83,500 people there, the largest Stones date in the country that tour.

"And we got a picture of that crowd from the upper deck in what

was left field. It's just such a powerful picture. It really gave a sense of the power and excitement this industry can create."

Though capacity for the Rock Hall con____ will___ limited to about 57,000, B____ ___ ____ ___ ___ity of ___ ___ ___ and $80__ ___ ___ ___ Ticketm___ ___ ___ ___ ___ placed ___

"Thes___ ___ ___ ___ are," Be___ ___ ___ these s___ ___ ___ know w___ ___ ___ ___ era set___ ___ ___ ___ we now ___ ___

Robb___ ___ Band, ___ ___ ___ acts to ___ ___ ___ the co___ ___ place ___ ___ ___ ___ also w___ ___ ___ measures ___

Though ___ ___ ing the sh___ ___ puts on i___ ___ weeks, th___ ___ landmar___

"I wou___ ___ he said. ___ created ___ ___ proud ___ ___ started ___ ___ big thi___ ___

"On ___ show i___ ___ in-a-li___

The___

motions when they presented a New Christy Minstrels/Four Freshmen show at Music Hall in 1966.

"We were in the clothing business when another clothing store in Ashtabula was giving away tickets to a ___ ___ ___ ___ing," Belkin

Above: Jules with the Cleveland International Film Festival team on Public Square, 2014
Below: Michael Stanley, Mike, Jules, Michael, and Barry Gabel at Cleveland Arts Prize 2015

134

Epilogue

In 1995, the decade-long quest to build the Rock & Roll Hall of Fame in Cleveland was reaching its climax, and the New York-based Rock Hall Foundation approached Jules to handle production for the epic opening event: The Concert for the Rock & Roll Hall of Fame. Over 30 major acts would share the stage at the all-star celebration in Cleveland Municipal Stadium.

Jules had been an active member of the Board of Directors of the Rock Hall since its inception, but he hadn't anticipated one day being asked to do the opening show. He was pleased—and flattered—that the New Yorkers entrusted his company to produce the internationally televised concert, and everyone at Belkin Productions was electrified at the prospect of being part of history. Jules, Michael, Barry, Stacey, Jamie and our entire crew meticulously ensured no detail would be overlooked.

After the final encore of the six-plus hour concert, we all breathed a sigh of relief: the eyes of the world were on Cleveland and it had been our job to ensure that everything went smoothly. And did it ever!

That night Jules felt he had reached the pinnacle of his career. The same stadium that had hosted the first World Series of Rock and countless other Belkin shows had just played its final rock concert, and it was one for the ages.

When Jules left the concert business in 2001, he never looked back. The Cleveland International Film Festival invited him to join their Board of Directors. They were struggling with a deficit situation and eagerly welcomed a businessman with Jules' experience. As the President of their Board for two terms, he steered them to financial stability and recruited talented, dedicated Board members.

Fran also moved on to become an active member of the Board of Directors at the Cleveland Institute of Art. She produced the film Tripped Up (trippedupmovie.com), about her son Steve's European travel competition which premiered at the Cleveland International Film Festival to sold out theaters, and she wrote this book. She and Jules occasionally work for their daughter's company, Jamie Belkin Events.

In 2015, Michael Belkin secretly nominated Jules and Mike for the Cleveland Arts Prize, and to everyone's astonishment, they won. The prize was a wonderful acknowledgment of all he and Mike had done for music in Cleveland, and for their overall support of the arts community. Michael Stanley gave the presentation speech at the ceremony and as always, he captivated the audience with his wit and charm.

GuitarMania

The GuitarMania public art project kicked off in 2002, initiated as a fundraiser for the Rock & Roll Hall of Fame. Dozens of artists submitted design concepts and then anxiously waited for a sponsor to choose and fund their design.

I collaborated with graphic designer Chris Hixson on "I'm with the Band", a mosaic and beaded design reimagining the guitar as a rock fan, wearing a t-shirt with one of my favorite rock expressions on the back: *If it's too loud, you're too old.*

Chris and I were ecstatic when Cleveland.com selected our design. Soon, the 10-foot guitar was delivered to my garage. I was stunned. I had no idea it would be *that* big.

I invited the Cleveland.com team to come string the beads for the belt. My daughter Jamie spent several weeks gluing on the black tiles while I struggled to create the intricate letters. Chris found the denim print tile and designed the belt buckle and World Series of Rock stage pass.

The team effort paid off, and our guitar was featured in the Plain Dealer and on the cover of the GuitarMania book before being auctioned to the highest bidder.

It was hard to say goodbye to our beloved guitar, but we were pleased it was purchased by a man who had been one of the first members of the Belkin Concert Club.

136

Photo: Bill Pappas

Biggest Rock Fans

A backstage pass...the most coveted item at any rock concert! At first they were fabric passes you stuck on your jeans—high on your thigh—until the bigger acts started making laminated stage passes worn on a lanyard. The artwork was usually from the album the band was promoting, and *always* they were super cool. KISS even put your photo on the back of the pass.

That exhilarating moment when we were handed our laminates and the security guard let us backstage never got old. I treasured the laminates and saved them, starting with the first one in 1975 from The Who. By 2016, I had quite a collection and wanted to give them to my two children. But how do you give someone a big bag of laminates?

If you're me, you find a way to turn them into art. I fashioned metal mesh into jeans and t-shirts and turned to Freeland Southerd at the Cleveland Institute of Art to weld the figures and make the bases, and then to Catherine Butler to craft the metal hands holding Bic lighters. Then I enjoyed a trip down concert memory lane while attaching the laminates. It was a challenging and fun project, culminating in Steve and Jamie's surprise when they came to the school and realized there was one for each of them.

Thank you...

Feb. 22-28 SCENE

Thanks - JULES & MIKE **BELKIN** for MAKING **CLEVELAND** the **ROCK 'N ROLL** CAPITAL of the **WORLD**!

the **BELKIN** Bros. & **WMMS** "Your CLEVELAND CONCERT CONNECTION"

To the talented **CHRIS HIXSON**, who organized and designed these stories and shirts into a funky yet exquisite book that is a joy to read. To my very special daughter **JAMIE** for smoothing many of my sentences into perfect prose. To my very special son **STEVE** who added so much personality to my pages. To my grandson **SAWYER**, who photographed many of the t-shirts and then planted me behind the camera and became my model. To **BARRY GABEL** for supporting me from day one: bringing me shirts I didn't have, remembering so much I forgot and writing our Foreword. To **WENDY STEIN** for inviting me to help backstage and for having the foresight to take some great Polaroids. To **JANET MACOSKA** for her encouragement and for always capturing the perfect concert image. To **AMBER KEMPTHORN** for her wonderful drawings. To **JUDIE ROSENMAN** for her friendship and encouragement. To **LAURA SEARS** for her insights, our index and credits. And finally, to my husband **JULES** who patiently endured my three-year obsession with this project.

Thank you to all the friends and family who shared their time and stories:

DIANA HAHN, STACEY HARPER, JERRY MIZER, MICHAEL STANLEY, MICHAEL BELKIN, GINA VERNACI, PHIL OBER, KATHY BARRIE, TOM EINHOUSE, JIMMY FOX, PAT MCKINLEY, LEO SCHLEICHER, CLAYTON TOWNSEND, SHERYL GORDON MARTINELLI, BILLY BASS, DENNY YOUNG, BONNIE LO CONTI, BILL PAPPAS, DAVID HELTON, BOB FERRELL, BRIAN FENDERBOSCH, BRIAN ZIMMERMAN, RICO MILLER, MITCHELL KAHAN, JEANNIE EMSER, PHYLLIS SLOAN, GAYLE BIBBE CRÈME, NICK CARIS, AND GERARDO ESPINOSA.
T-SHIRT MANNEQUINS: SAWYER OPALICH, JAMIE BELKIN, FRAN BELKIN, JULES BELKIN

" How about a holiday card with our old Belkin t-shirts? "

Our grandchildren loved the idea for our annual greeting, so we searched through the archives and picked our favorite shirts for them to wear, and it made a fun card for 2013.

VINTAGE BELKIN →

belkin PRODUCTIONS EST. 1966

Simon & Garfunkel July 19, 1983 Akron Rubber Bowl

BELKIN AND THE "BOSS"
BRUCE SPRINGSTEEN & THE E STREET BAND
COMPLETELY SOLD OUT!

BELKIN PRODUCTIONS

TOLEDO SPEEDWAY JAM FOREIGNER LOVERBOY TRIUMPH DONNY IRIS June 27th, 1982

WORLD SERIES ROCK

SOLD OUT

SAWYER

NIKKI

DYLAN

MAX

BEAU

Index

And finally, our all-time favorite t-shirts that were designed by others. We never got to make a shirt for Bowie, but his merchandise was so cool I always bought some. And Jules still enjoys his Aerosmith shirt designed by Joey Mars for the 1996 Get a Grip tour.

'When you're a promoter, there's just something about walking into a full house. And it's not necessarily the monetary aspect, either. It's more the fact that this is something you created, something you built. It's the way we feel about a good concert. It took a lot of effort to put it together, it was successful and a lot of pleasure was given to the people in those seats. '

Jules Belkin

Quoted in Akron
Beacon Journal,
April 20, 1980

Copyrights & Photo Credits